Beauty Masks & Scrubs

ELAINE STAVERT

Beauty Masks & Scrubs

GUILD OF MASTER CRAFTSMAN PUBLICATIONS

First published in 2010 by
Guild of Master Craftsman Publications Ltd
Castle Place, 166 High Street,
Lewes, East Sussex BN7 1XU

ISBN: 978-1-86108-692-1

Associate Publisher: Jonathan Bailey
Production Manager: Jim Bulley
Managing Editor: Gerrie Purcell
Editor: Beth Wicks
Managing Art Editor: Gilda Pacitti
Designer: Rob Janes

Set in Gill Sans

Colour origination by GMC Reprographics
Printed and bound by Hing Yip Printing Co. Ltd in China

Please note that imperial measurements throughout are
approximate conversions from metric. When following
the instructions, use either the metric or the imperial
measurements, do not mix units. For further information
refer to the table on page 148.

Why we love masks & scrubs

Mother Nature has given us some precious gifts,
to rejuvenate the skin and provide a face lift.
With fruit, eggs and honey, cow's milk or cream,
with regular use you'll become a beauty queen.

Soothing, cleansing and enriching the skin,
clay masks with fruit powders are most definitely in.
To enhance your pores and reduce fine lines,
all you need are ingredients and a few minutes of time.

So at the end of the day when you grind to a halt,
scrub your skin with sugar or Epsom salt.
It will buff up your skin to a wonderful shine,
washing away all the dirt and the grime.

Have a go at creating unique skin care,
for family and friends to enjoy and to share.
Soon you'll find out why it's not a task,
to make your own beauty scrubs and masks.

Contents

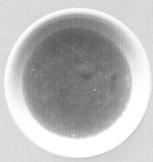

3

4

5

6

11

12

13

14

15   16   17   18

23   24   25   26

19

20

21

22

27

28

29

30

A history of bathing

No life form can survive without water; our bodies are made up of approximately 75 per cent H₂O and many cultures' beliefs feature water at the moment of creation. As well as cleansing and refreshing, **bathing in water gives us a feeling of comfort and security, peace and contentment, perhaps subconsciously reminding us of the protective time in our mother's womb.**

Since prehistoric times humans and animals have enjoyed the therapeutic and curative powers of mineral waters. The act of bathing has meant different things to many cultures over the centuries, with some people completely scouring and cleaning their bodies in rivers, springs, pools, wells and reservoirs, while others decline to dip even a toe into water. The spiritual energy of water was thought to be one of the divine forces of nature which would heal, cleanse and purify the spirit. Bathing in water was, therefore, initially used in religious ceremonies to cleanse the spirit and for marking the rites of passage, rather than for cleaning the body.

Spas and hot springs

The Egyptians were prolific bathers, spending hours on their ablutions. They bathed at home in a separate room in the house using perfumed creams made from lime and oil, after which they smothered their bodies with aromatic oils to nourish and protect their skin.

Left: A morning Aarti (Hindu ritual) beside the River Ganges in India.
Water continues to play an important role in many religions.

For the Greeks, bathing was a social occasion for the men with individual hip baths situated around a main pool where they would chat, play dice, and even enjoy a drink or a snack. There were also rooms for cold and warm baths, which were similar although less sophisticated than the later Roman baths. For the wealthy upper-classes, baths were also available in Greek gymnasiums where they would go to build and maintain their strength for the outdoor exercise fields. Here men oiled and dusted their naked bodies before exercising, playing ball games, or wrestling. Afterwards, they would scrape away dirt, sweat and excess oil from their skin with a curved metal tool called a strigil, before washing off the excess with unheated water from a bath or basin. This method of washing was popular before the availability of effective soaps.

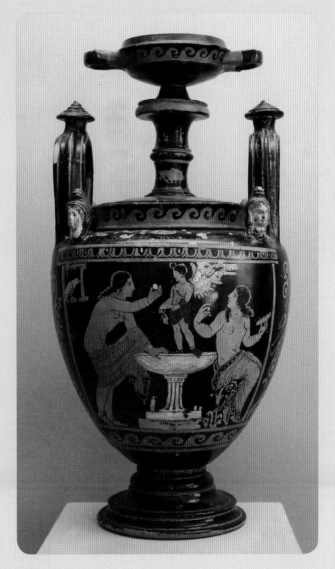

Below: Groups of men continue to gather to socialise and play games while bathing at public baths such as this thermal spa in Budapest, Hungary.

Above: The men didn't have all the bathing fun in ancient history. This painted vase, from around 340BC, shows two women washing at a fountain in which Eros, the ancient Greek god of love, stands.

BEAUTY MASKS & SCRUBS

The Roman baths

While the focus at Greek baths was education and sport, the baths and spas in Roman times were a place for bathing, socializing, relaxation and pleasure, all integral parts of daily life. People from all classes and walks of life, both rich and poor, slaves and masters, would spend hours at a time at the baths socializing with friends and associates. The Romans were so fond of their baths that they built them wherever they went throughout their conquests across Europe, including the famous baths in the appropriately named city of Bath, England. Many wealthy Romans also had their own private baths in addition to using the public baths.

Some of the greatest advancements in bathing were made by the Romans. For them splashing, soaking, steaming and oiling their bodies was part of everyday life. Medical publications of the time advocated adopting a healthy regime as both prevention and cure of the unknown and mysterious illnesses that could strike. Bathing featured greatly in these writings.

Left: The word lavender stems from the latin word lavare, meaning 'to wash'. Ancient Greeks and Romans frequently used lavender to scent their bath water. It remains a popular fragrance in skincare products today.

Right: Sponges and Strigils (1879), by the Victorian painter Sir Lawrence Alma Tadema, shows a romanticized view of female bathers in an Ancient Roman bath. The woman on the right is using the traditional strigil.

Medicinal bathing for all was therefore considered to be of great importance. Physicians prescribed cold water baths, sweating and vapour treatments for various illnesses. Masseurs would also practise at the baths offering their services as a preventative treatment. It is clear that the Romans understood the connection between health and bathing.

Below: A floorplan of the old baths in Pompeii shows just how complex these buildings were. Different areas were allocated to a caldarium (hot bath), tepidarium (warm bath) and frigidarium (cold bath), as well as separate areas for women and servants.

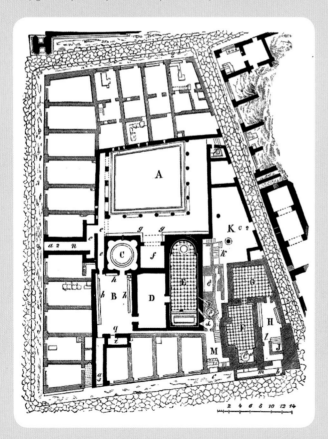

Public baths began to decline in the 5th century due to the fall of the Roman Empire and the growth of Christianity. At that time the church believed that the uninhibited behaviour that occurred at these baths promoted immorality, as well as the spread of disease. Christians actively sought to close down many public baths, resulting in a decline in public bathing and the return to the great unwashed.

Bath spa

The city of Bath, England, is built on top of three mineral-rich hot thermal springs where archaeological evidence of human activity has been discovered going back as far as 8,000 years. A hot steamy swamp was probably not the most inviting place for humans to live, so there was probably no settlement in this area all those years ago. However, legend has it that the leprous Prince Bladud was cured of his illness after bathing in these therapeutic waters. He was so grateful for his restoration to health that he founded the city in 863BC.

The Romans discovered the site in around AD43 and went on to build a healing shrine with a reservoir and a series of baths and temples, dedicated to their goddess Sulis Minerva, in the city. People came from right across Britain and Europe to visit the spas. Even members of royalty and the nobility would visit Bath to 'take in the waters' to ease ailments, such as rheumatism, gout, lumbago, sciatica and neuritis.

In early 17th century England, spas also opened at Tunbridge Wells, Epsom and Harrogate. Dr William Oliver's *Practical Dissertation on Bath Water* published in 1707, further helped to raise the popularity of bathing in thermal waters.

Above: A view of the Roman baths at Bath, UK, taken around 1900. The Victorians, who were passionate about history, had expanded the baths' buildings and added statues of Roman emperors.

Above right: A statue of the legendary King Bladud overlooks the Sacred Pool of Sulis, named after the Celtic goddess Sulis Minerva.

Right: Under the caldarium (or hot room) at Bath, UK. Hot air circulated in the spaces between the pillars which supported the floor, in an early form of underfloor heating.

Thermae Bath Spa

Towards the end of the 20th century, the Roman baths and pump rooms in Bath became one of the UK's leading tourist attractions. This re-established interest in thermal spas creating a demand for the reopening of therapeutic spa facilities. In 2006, the Thermae Bath Spa opened combining modern facilities with a tradition of well-being dating back over 2,000 years. The spa uses the hot, mineral-rich waters from the Kings Spring, the Hetling Spring and the Cross Spring. The addition of the contemporary New Royal Bath also offers a state-of-the-art rooftop pool overlooking the historical city of Bath.

During the construction of the Thermae Bath Spa extensive drilling was carried out to discover more about the thermal waters. While the source remains a mystery, the water was found to contain over 42 minerals and trace elements, including sulphate, calcium, chloride, sodium, bicarbonate, magnesium, silica and iron. The temperature and flow continues to be monitored and remains relatively constant with only small degrees of variations.

The Thermae Bath Spa provides a unique experience; residents and visitors to Bath can now finally bathe again in Britain's original and only natural thermal spa, soaking in therapeutic natural waters on a site rich in ancient spa history.

Thermal springs

A thermal spring contains water that is much hotter than the surrounding atmosphere. The water permeates deep into the crust of the earth where it obtains its heat, then rises to the surface bringing with it gases and precious minerals. These mineral-rich waters are often purified and bottled as mineral water, or bathed in for their therapeutic effects.

Iceland is a country famous for its substantial amount of volcanic activity, geysers and thermal springs. The well-known geothermic bathing spa, The Blue Lagoon, near Reykjavik, is rich in sulphur with a deep aqua colour and a milky appearance due to the salts, silica and algae in the water. Bathing in the Blue Lagoon is deeply relaxing, nourishing, cleansing, exfoliating and healing. The waters are reknowned for their beneficial effects on the skin, in particular for soothing psoriasis, and for relieving stress and tension.

Below: The geothermal seawater in The Blue Lagoon, Iceland, has been shown to heal particular skin conditions and draws visitors from all over the world.

Above: A nineteenth century advertisement extolling the benefits of exercise, herbs and hydrotherapy treatments.

Spas

A spa is a tranquil retreat which uses water – hydrotherapy – for holistic, personal care or health treatments as either prevention or relief from various ailments. The treatments available generally include massage, body wraps, facials, reiki, aromatherapy, water therapy, reflexology and acupuncture, to name but a few. The tranquil environment also offers a place to rebalance, alleviate stress, and to encourage general well-being and peace.

In the months following the First World War, thousands of wounded soldiers were rehabilitated in British spa towns such as Bath. In 1948, the health authorities started to provide water-cure treatments at the spas on prescription, until they eventually built their own pool. With the start of the National Health Service and the availability of free medicine, interest in the spas declined steadily and they began to close.

However in recent years, spas and complementary health treatments have once again gained popularity. Affordable flights and an increase in leisure time have made trips to natural springs in exotic places an option for many people. Destinations such as the Dead Sea in Israel and the traditional baths of Eastern Europe draw thousands of health-seeking visitors every year, while most towns have their own 'spa' in the form of a beauty salon.

But you don't need to break the bank or fly across the world to enjoy a spa-style treatment. Simply grab a few ingredients and a bit of 'me-time' and you'll soon have a therapeutic haven in your own home.

Ancient Egyptian beauty

What were the secrets of the natural beauties of the ancient past? And can we re-create these ourselves in a world full of chemical-laden creams, lotions and potions that promise the earth but cost a small fortune?

The Ancient Egyptians were renowned for their extensive skin and body preparations. They paid particular attention to their appearance and used expensive perfumes and potions to scent their skin. Plant oils and extracts were used to smooth their skin and to decorate their bodies in a similar fashion to today's makeup.

In those times, there were no large pharmaceutical companies churning out bottles of potions, so the Egyptians had to use whatever was at hand, including the various ingredients brought into the country via the many trading routes. Herbs, plants, spices, flowers, gums, resins, oils, fats and flowers were all used in creation of the numerous perfumes and unguents (soothing herbal salves, ointments or preparations used for healing and for sexual encounters).

The dry heat from the Egyptian desserts made the use of oils necessary for keeping skin soft and supple. Even the workers, would be given unscented inexpensive vegetable oil, such as sengen, castor or sesame oil, as part of their day's pay as it was considered such a necessity.

Left: Queen Cleopatra was renowned for her beauty in ancient Egyptian times.

Above: Various vessels which would have contained minerals and ointments placed in an Egyptian tomb for use in the afterlife.

Below: A carved bowl in the form of a gazelle, used to hold kohl.

Queen Cleopatra and other women of her time would use honey and salt to condition their skin, or a cream consisting of oil and chalk for cleansing and exfoliation, very similar to our modern-day scrubs and masks. They would also add milk to their baths, which is rich in AHAs (Alpha Hydroxy Acids) ideal for exfoliating and cleansing the skin – try it yourself, you will be amazed at the results. Many of these renowned recipes have been passed down through history and are still known and used today.

Egyptian women also decorated their bodies with a form of makeup. They focused particularly on their eyes, emphasizing their size and shape. The wall paintings in the tomb of Nefertari, Queen of Ramasses II, show a dark hue over her cheek bones indicating the makeup that she wore. The red colour was usually obtained from red ochre, a mineral pigment found in the desert. As well as ochre, additional minerals were used to create the limited range of colours – green from malachite, carbonate of copper and galena, and black from a form of lead sulphide. Kohl was made from soot mixed with a fixative. Today, mineral makeup is all the rage, perhaps we are coming back round full circle.

It is human instinct to want to look our best and to preserve our youth for as long as possible. We cannot defy the ageing process, but we can take five minutes out of our day and, instead of throwing away leftover cucumber, strawberries or tomatoes, or that last tablespoon of milk or yoghurt, use it on our skin to enhance beauty, minimize wrinkles, and keep our skin soft and silky smooth.

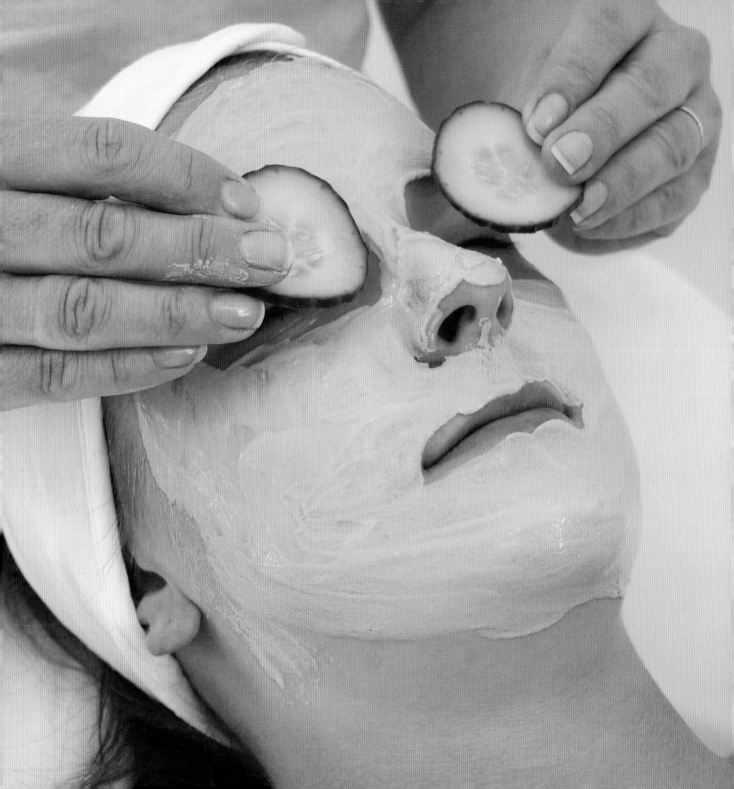

Basic Techniques

Equipment and materials

You will not need any complicated equipment to make the recipes in this book; in fact, you will probably have most of it in your kitchen already.

Even the raw ingredients are easily obtained from the growing number of mail order 'cosmetic supplies' companies (see suppliers on page 149).

Aloe vera

Oils

Honey

Food blender

Herbs

Pipette

Plastic containers

Exfoliants

Spatula

Clay

Measuring scales

Non-metallic measuring jug

Measuring spoons

Fresh fruit and veg

Small mixing dish

Small whisk

Spoon

Kitchen knife

Juicer

Herbs and spices

Salt

23

Face and body scrubs

Scrubs are extremely easy to make and can be made quickly with simple ingredients from your kitchen cupboard. They are also very beneficial for your skin, removing dead skin cells, unblocking pores, and improving circulation. A great way to reveal fresh, healthy skin.

What is a scrub?

A scrub or polish is a suspension of coarse natural granules or ingredients in an emollient such as oil. This mixture is massaged or rubbed vigorously into the body to exfoliate or slough away any dead skin cells and dirt. It is then washed off with water to expose a soft and supple layer of new skin cells and silky soft skin. The oil in the scrub conditions and moisturizes the skin, while the abrasive ingredients invigorate the body and improve the circulation of the blood and lymphatic system.

Benefits of a scrub

Cleaning and exfoliating

The natural abrasive ingredients in body scrubs slough away old skin, dirt and oil from the outer skin layers. This unclogs blocked pores to expose the skin's deeper, healthier layers and reveal cleaner, fresher and younger looking skin.

Some readily-available exfoliating ingredients include (top) ground almonds, (bottom right) brown sugar and (bottom left) oatbran.

Moisturizing

Some of the harsh ingredients in commercial skin-care products can strip the body of natural oils, leaving it dry and itchy. Body scrubs made with oil, on the other hand, moisturize and nurture dry, flaky or parched skin. There are numerous beneficial oils to choose from, a selection of which can be used in body scrubs. These can be found in the section on oils starting on page 78.

Cellulite and circulation

Body scrubs can also have cellulite combating properties. Cellulite is the term used to describe areas of your body that have a dimpled appearance of orange peel, caused by fatty deposits just below the surface of the skin. Vigorously rubbing body scrubs into these affected areas increases the blood flow to the skin and improves the areas of cellulite, while firming and smoothing the skin.

Aromatherapy

When added to body scrubs, aromatherapy oils provide added beneficial therapeutic effects, such as relaxation or stimulation. For more information refer to the essential oils section starting on page 67.

When to use a scrub

- To keep your skin glowing and healthy apply a body scrub regularly, either once a week or every two weeks. Do not use it more frequently as too much scrubbing can damage young, new skin cells. If you have sensitive skin, use a gentle abrasive, such as oats, fine sugar or salt, as opposed to larger grains.

- Before a leg wax to remove the dead skin cells and make epilation (the removal of the hair) easier.

- Before applying a self-tan. Removal of the dead skin cells will create a smoother skin texture and therefore help to provide a more even tan.

- After exposure to the sun. During the hot summer months, your skin can quickly become dry and flaky. Body scrubs will give your skin a silky luminous glow. However, do not use it on sunburnt skin.

- Before a body wrap or mud treatment to open the skin's pores and prepare your skin for your wrap

- As part of your facial routine to brighten and even skin tone, or before using a face mask.

Scrub components

Exfoliating material

This is the ingredient that provides the scrubbiness to your scrub. Natural ingredients, such as sea salt, sugar, ground oats, seeds, coffee grounds etc., can all be used to exfoliate the skin. Scrubs vary in texture and strength depending on the desired effect. Coarse grains in a body scrub, for example salt, would be too rough to use on the delicate skin of the face; whereas a gentle exfoliating ingredient, such as oats, would be too soft to use on the hard skin of the feet. A number of exfoliating materials and their uses can be found on pages 42–47.

Oil or emollient

Unless you are making a dry scrub, you need to add oil to your scrub. The oil acts as a lubricant to the exfoliating ingredient, ensuring the scrub slides easily over your skin. Without the oil the scrub would be dry, coarse and rough, therefore potentially damaging to the skin. Information on the different oils that can be used in your scrub can be found in the essential oils section starting on page 67.

Herbs

Powdered herbs, such as ginseng, green tea or comfrey, can provide additional therapeutic benefits to your scrub. They may also help with skin conditions or ailments. See pages 54–59 for more information on herbs.

Clays and mud

Various clays or mud can be added to your scrubs. These ingredients cleanse the skin, draw out toxins, provide nutrient rich minerals and help to enhance the texture of your skin.

Fruit and vegetables

The active properties in certain fruits and vegetables, for example strawberries and tomatoes, also help to remove dead skin cells. Fresh fruits or spray-dried powdered fruits can both be used, see pages 64–66 for further information.

Essential oils

Aromatherapy (essential) oils are renowned for their therapeutic benefits. These oils vary in their effects, they can be detoxing, soothing or stimulating. Select the essential oils suitable for your scrub by using the chart on page 77. Fragrance oils can also be added for scent, although they do not have any of the therapeutic benefits.

Powdered mango

Making a dry scrub

A dry scrub prepared and ready for use.

1 Measure or weigh all the dry ingredients, then place them in a mixing bowl.

2 Thoroughly mix the ingredients together with a spoon or small whisk.

3 Either store the dry scrub in a container for future use or use it straight away by adding an activator, such as water, milk or oil.

Making an oil scrub

An oil-based scrub ready for application.

1 Weigh out the oils and blend them together with your essential oils and/or fragrance.

2 Weigh the exfoliating ingredient, such as sea salt, sugar, coffee grounds etc.

3 Mix the exfoliating ingredient and oil together.

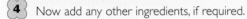 Now add any other ingredients, if required.

 Mix well, then place in a storage container.

Alternative method

Alternatively, simply fill a container with exfoliating material, pour in the oil and mix. You will know when you have added enough oil as a film of oil will appear on the top of the exfoliating ingredient after the scrub has been left to settle for a while.

How to apply scrubs

With all scrubs and masks, if you have allergies or sensitive skin make sure that you do a test patch first before applying them.

Applying a body scrub

For easy application a body scrub is best applied to clean damp or wet skin. Stand in the shower or bath and apply the scrub with your hands. Massage it into your skin using circular motions, starting with the legs, thighs and buttocks. If you wish to scrub your stomach, make sure that you gently scrub in a clockwise direction to avoid upsetting your digestion. Carry on up the body as far as the neck scrubbing upwards towards the heart. The scrub should then be washed off with water, before applying moisturizer or lotion if desired.

Do not apply a body scrub to your face unless it is specified for use on the face, as the exfoliating material used for the body is usually too abrasive to use on such a delicate area of skin.

Applying a face scrub

Pin your hair back or use a headband to keep your hair away from your face. Cleanse your face and remove all traces of make up, then dampen it with water. Apply the face scrub starting at your neck and chin. Use soft circular strokes to massage the scrub upwards and outwards over the cheeks. Move up the face to the upper lip, but avoiding the tender skin on the lips themselves. Massage well in and around the crevices of the nose area, an area that often contains blackheads and blocked pores. Finally, move up to the temples and forehead avoiding the eye lids. Gently rinse the scrub off with water, keeping your eyes closed. You may now wish to apply a face mask. When you have finished, apply a moisturizer to your skin.

An exfoliating body scrub

Note: Do not shave or apply any astringent or alcohol-based products to the face after applying a scrub as this could sting or irritate the skin.

Applying a hand scrub

It is a good idea to keep a hand scrub by your kitchen sink to remind you to exfoliate your hands every week or two. Simply wet your hands, apply the scrub and rub your hands together. Then rinse the scrub away with warm water.

Applying a foot scrub

Soak your feet in a bowl of warm water for 5–10 minutes. When the feet are soft and warm, massage the scrub over the soles of your feet, heels, ankles and toes. Rinse the scrub away with warm water, then pat your feet dry with a towel. Alternatively, you may wish to apply a foot scrub while you are lying in a shallow bath with your foot raised out of the water. If you apply a scrub whilst standing in a shower, be very careful that you do not slip over.

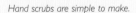

Hand scrubs are simple to make.

An exfoliating salt-based foot scrub.

Masks and wraps

Face or body masks are usually part of a costly salon or spa treatment, yet they can easily be made from inexpensive and readily available dried or fresh ingredients. Many of which can be found in your refrigerator or kitchen larder, such as fruit, eggs, vegetable oils, dairy produce or honey.

A mask is a mixture of ingredients rich in minerals or vitamins which are usually, but not exclusively, applied to the face to cleanse and smooth the skin, tighten and refine pores, remove excess oil, or nurture the skin. They can be made from fresh or dry ingredients, such as clay, powdered herbs, spray-dried fruit or powdered milk.

Benefits of a face mask

The benefits obtained by a face mask depend on the various ingredients used. Various ingredients deeply cleanse and condition your skin, rehydrate, exfoliate, even the skin tone, soothe sunburn, and moisturize dry or mature skin. While other ingredients can help to heal acne, scars or pigmentation, increase the blood circulation and stimulate the lymphatic system. Face masks are also a good way to help remove blackheads, whiteheads, spots and blemishes, while brightening the skin and leaving it taught, refreshed and youthful.

When to use a mask

- Once a week, use a face mask to improve the condition and texture of your skin. Using a mask regularly can make the difference between having just good skin or really fantastic skin.

- During stressful times in your life when the pressure begins to show on your face.

- To improve the condition of your skin for a very important occasion or celebration. However, never use a new mask just before an important event. You do not want to wake up on the big day and find that you have had an allergic reaction to an ingredient.

Note: It is not advisable to use a face mask if you have broken or infected skin or particularly sensitive skin.

Types of mask

There is a wide range of masks suitable for various skin types. When making your own, consider your skin type and what you are looking to achieve. The key types of masks are:

Clay
These masks are particularly good for drawing out impurities from the skin and giving a really deep cleanse.

Egg
Egg white is a good base for a mask to which you can add other ingredients. Egg yolk moisturizes and nurtures dry skin.

Dairy
The natural mild acids in full-fat milk, cream or yoghurt gently cleanse, exfoliate, soothe and soften the skin.

Fruit and vegetable
The enzymes in fresh and powdered fruit provide gentle exfoliation, whilst the multitudes of vitamins can brighten and illuminate the skin. Citrus fruits, such as lemons, are particularly good for oily skin, cucumber is cooling and toning, whereas avocado is highly moisturizing.

Honey
Honey is a valuable base to use in a mask due to its anti-bacterial, antiseptic, anti-fungal and moisturizing properties. Other ingredients can be added to further enhance the benefits of a honey mask.

Herbal
Herbs have a multitude of different therapeutic benefits which can help with minor aliments. There are numerous herbs that are obtained in powdered form, including green tea, lemon peel and peppermint.

Seaweed
Anti-inflammatory, healing and detoxifying, seaweed body wraps or face masks are luxury treatments found in many of the top spas and salons.

Chocolate (cocoa powder)
The cocoa solids in chocolate are extremely high in anti-oxidants which help to prevent cell damage.

Buttermilk powder and sliced cucumber. Both fresh and dried ingredients can be included in your masks.

Using activators

Dry or powdered masks are 'activated' or hydrated by adding a liquid such as oil and mixing them to a thick paste, so that they adhere to the skin. Activators you can use include water, fruit juice, milk, cream, yoghurt, oil, massage oil, honey, floral waters, herbal tinctures or brine (sea salt dissolved in water).

The activator you choose to use will depend on your skin type and your personal preference. For detailed information on the various activators, refer to the ingredients section starting on page 40.

How much to use

The amount of activator required depends on the ingredients used to make the mask, the viscosity of the activator (for instance, you may well need more honey than water), and your personal preference – some people prefer a thick mask, while others prefer to apply just a thin covering.

As a guide, for a face mask add ½–1½ teaspoon (2.5–7.5ml) of activator to one heaped teaspoon (5ml) of dry mixture. For a hand, foot, leg, hair or body wrap, simply add enough activator to your dry ingredients to make a thick mixture. Remember that some clays or particular ingredients will have greater water absorption properties than others, so add a little at a time until the desired thickness is obtained. The aim is to achieve a smooth, thick paste that will adhere to the skin.

Adding an activator to a dry mask mix.

Notes: If your dry mask is too thin and runny, you have added too much activator. Leave the mixture for 10–20 minutes before using, so that the excess liquid has the opportunity to be absorbed by the dry material and may thicken to create the right consistency.

Once mixed with an activator to the right consistency, a mask should be used immediately, at least within 10 minutes, otherwise it will dry out and deteriorate. Therefore only mix up the amount that you will use on each occasion.

Making a dry mask or wrap

A simple dry mask, ready for storage.

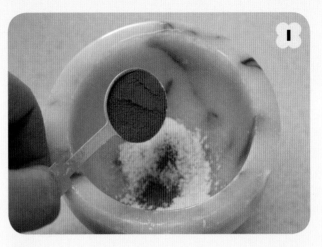

1 Measure out the dry ingredients, such as clay, powdered herbs, powdered fruit or powdered milk into a mixing bowl.

2 Thoroughly mix the ingredients together using a spoon or a small hand whisk

3 Either transfer the mixture into a storage container to be stored somewhere dry away from direct heat and light, or mix it up straight away with an activator of your choice.

Making a mask with fresh fruit or vegetables

A fresh fruit or vegetable mask needs to be used straightaway.

1 Finely chop the fruit or vegetable ingredients using a kitchen knife, then place in a bowl.

2 Using an electric hand blender, purée the ingredients until the mixture is as smooth as possible. A lumpy mask will be difficult to stick to your skin and may slip off.

3 You may wish to add other ingredients to your puree so as to make the paste thicker and easier to apply. Suggestions include powdered fruit, powdered milk, clay, yoghurt, honey, or powdered honey, ground almonds, or even whipped cream.

How to apply a face mask

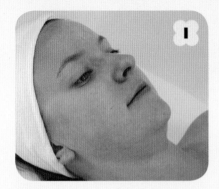

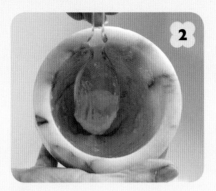

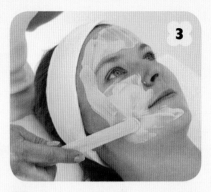

1 Tie your hair back to keep it off your face, then thoroughly cleanse your face. You may wish to apply a face scrub before using your mask to remove any dead skin cells.

2 If you are using a dry mask you will need to hydrate the powder with an activator to create a thick paste.

3 Using a paintbrush, make up brush, wooden stick or your fingers, apply the mask in soft circular motions to the neck and face, avoiding the eyes and lips.

4 Lie still and relax. Leave your mask on for approximately 15 minutes. If you are using a clay mask, make sure that it has completely dried before removing it to obtain the full benefits.

5 You may wish to cover your eyes with cooling slices of cucumber, cold used tea bags, or a lavender bag.

6 When the time is up, remove your mask with warm water and a flannel or muslin cloth. Ensure that all traces of the mask are removed. Then gently pat your face dry with a towel and moisturize.

Body masks and wraps

A clay or mud body wrap is essentially the same as a face mask with the same beneficial properties, except that it is applied to a larger area of skin, often following the application of a body scrub. Body wraps are also used to slim and tone the body, firm the skin, or to relax the muscles. When used on a regular basis, they have been shown to help people lose weight. Clay body wraps are also particularly helpful for stimulating the metabolic system, thereby speeding up the body's ability to remove toxins and waste products.

When to use body wraps

- As a general detox and skin conditioning treatment.

- If you are dieting to help lose those inches.

- If you have lost weight or after having a child, to tighten up and tone flabby skin.

- To help reduce the appearance of cellulite.

Note: Do not use a body wrap if you have high blood pressure or you are claustrophobic.

Foot and leg masks

After using a foot scrub, a foot or leg mask softens and soothes dry, tired feet or conditions the skin before a self-tan. Extending the mask up the calves also helps to relieve aching legs.

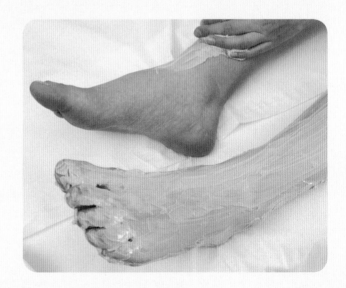

How to apply a body wrap

To obtain the best results exfoliate your body with a scrub before applying a body wrap (see page 30).

To make up the wrap, add warm water (or brine – a mixture of salt and warm water) and a few teaspoons of oil to the dry mask mixture, then mix to a thick paste.

This is a messy business, so stand in an empty bath and apply the mixture to your body, including your neck and face if you wish. You can either use your hands, a clean paintbrush, or a kitchen spatula.

Next, wrap yourself tightly in old sheets, bandages or even an emergency foil blanket, making sure that your arms are covered. The tightness of the bandages or sheets helps to compress soft tissue. Further cover yourself with warm towels – the key to this treatment is warmth. Keep your skin as warm as possible, so that your pores remain open and you sweat the toxins away, while absorbing the wrap's nutrients.

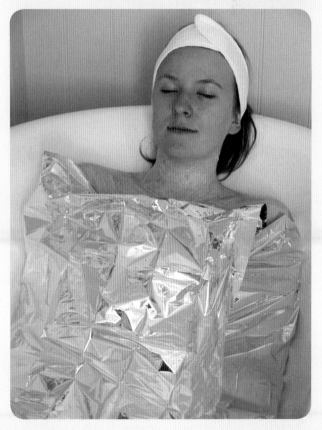

Lie still in the empty bath and relax for 45–60 minutes, before showering the mixture off. Pat dry and follow the treatment with an all-over mositurizer.

Note: It is not advisable to dash about or play sports after this relaxing treatment. Simply drink plenty of water and sit quietly for a few hours.

Basic Ingredients

Exfoliants

The main ingredient in your face or body scrub is your exfoliant. To 'exfoliate' your skin simply means to scrub your skin with an abrasive material, thereby stripping away old skin cells from the outer layer of your skin and stimulating the production of collagen. This rejuvenates your skin to reveal new cells and silky smooth skin. It can also help to diminish the appearance of fine lines or wrinkles and ease spotty skin and mild acne.

There are many natural ingredients that can be used to exfoliate your skin. Some are more abrasive than others, so select your exfoliant according to the action or purpose required. Many ingredients, such as pumice or loofah, are available in different grounds or grain sizes; the more finely ground the material the more suitable it is for using on your face. If you are unsure whether your exfoliant is suitable for your face, ask your supplier.

Dairy products and particular fruits, such as lemon, strawberry and apple, can also help with the exfoliation of dead skin cells. More information on these can be found in the fruit and vegetable section (page 64) and the dairy sections (page 62).

Apricot shells (ground)
Prunus armeniaca
Apricot shells are apricot stones that have been finely grounded. They can be added to face or body scrubs for a highly exfoliating gritty texture that will leave your skin feeling fresh and invigorated.

Almonds (ground)
Prunus dulcis
Ground almonds soften and nourish your skin providing a very gentle exfoliation. Regular applications can also prevent blackheads and spots. Due to their very gentle action, ground almonds are particularly suited to facial scrubs and for use on sensitive skin.

Bamboo powder
Bambusa vulgaris
Bamboo is a rapidly growing versatile plant with a hollow stem. The sap, leaves and shavings are used in Chinese medicine to ease fevers and infections, while bamboo powder is rich in both minerals and silica which are beneficial for wrinkles and acne. Used with other exfoliating materials, clays or mud it can create exotic face or body scrubs.

Coffee grounds

Coffea arabica

Coffee makes a wonderful exfoliating ingredient with which to stimulate and tone the skin. A coffee body scrub smells divine and leaves your skin feeling zingy, alive and ready for action. Coffee body scrubs are also frequently used to help reduce cellulite. Instead of throwing away left-over coffee grounds, mix them with oil and use them in the shower for an effective body scrub, at the same time saving yourself a fortune at the spa. Alternatively, when you are in the kitchen, grab a handful, then mix with a little cooking oil and exfoliate your hands. You can also add salt for extra scrubbiness – mix one part salt to four parts of coffee, if desired.

Cranberry seeds

Vaccinium macrocarpon

Obtained from cranberry fruits, the seeds gently exfoliate the skin and are a great addition to facial scrubs. Add a few drops of mandarin orange essential oil for a seasonal pick-me-up.

Epsom salts

Magnesium sulphate

Epsom salts take their name from the small English town where salt was produced by boiling down the local mineral-rich water. The salts have wonderful detoxification properties and are popular for flushing out toxins, taking the sting out of insect bites, drawing out splinters, promoting circulation, and deep cleansing the skin. They are highly exfoliating, ideal for use in body scrubs. Alternatively, dissolve some salts in warm water and use as a detoxifying activator for face masks or body wraps. Soaking in an Epsom salt bath can also increase your magnesium levels. This has many benefits including easing muscle pain, relieving stress and insomnia.

Coffee grounds

Epsom salts

Loofah

Luffa

Loofah sponges are the dried interior tissues of tropical gourd-like vegetables grown on the vine in Africa and Asia. They can be used whole as a bath sponge or finely shredded into strands of fibrous material and added to scrubs. Loofahs can be used in combination with other exfoliants with different textures, such as pumice or salt, to make an excellent foot scrub. Very finely shredded loofah can also be used on the face.

Oats/oatmeal/oat bran

Avena sativa

Oats are the seed of a cereal grain, the extract of which is used in many topical skin-care applications for eczema and psoriasis and to help manage dry or itchy skin conditions. Oats ground to a fine texture in a food processor can also be used in facial scrubs. They provide a gentle exfoliation leaving the skin soft and silky, making them well-suited to sensitive skin.

Peach stones (ground)

Prunus persica

Ground from the stones of peach fruits, this exfoliant is a fabulous addition to either face or body scrubs. If you are unable to obtain peach stones, ground apricot will do the job just as well.

Pumice

Pumice

Pumice stones are pieces of solidified, frothy volcanic stone that were shot out of a volcano during an eruption. As the stone solidifies, multitudes of holes are created, giving it a sponge-like appearance. The myriad of holes makes pumice an incredibly light material which can float on water. Pumice is available in various sized grains of ground powder. It is a very useful natural abrasive and exfoliant and therefore particularly good for foot, hand or body scrubs. If using an oil-based scrub, mix it thoroughly before application to re-distribute any pumice which may have sunk down to the bottom.

Shredded loofah

Ground peach stones

Pumice powder

Poppy seeds

Papaver orientale

Poppy seeds are smooth round seeds obtained from the poppy flower which can be added to body or facial scrubs. They provide gentle exfoliation and make an interesting texture when added to other exfoliating materials.

Raspberry seeds

Rubus idaeus

Obtained from raspberry fruits, these small soft seeds are used to provide gentle exfoliation for the face and are a perfect ingredient for a fruity facial scrub. Combine them with clay powder and powdered raspberry, mango or banana to create a fruit salad scrub.

Salt

Sodium chloride

Salt is something that we probably all now take for granted as it's so readily available. Yet throughout history salt was one of the most sought-after and precious commodities. Sea salt is a mineral created by the evaporation of sea water and has been viewed as a valuable ingredient for thousands of years. Rich in beneficial minerals, such as magnesium, silicon, potassium and calcium, sea salt can be used to make therapeutic bath salts or soaks and is a wonderful exfoliating ingredient for foot and body scrubs. When applied to the skin, salt helps to purify and soften the skin, as well as ease aching muscles. However, it is highly abrasive and therefore not recommended for use on the face.

Poppy seeds

Raspberry seeds

Coarse sea salt

Dead Sea salts

Maris sal

For thousands of years, kings and queens have travelled from far and wide to bathe in the Dead Sea, situated between Israel and Jordan. Once part of the ocean, the Dead Sea, is now a lake containing extremely high levels of salt and minerals. The levels of salinity in this mineral-rich water are so high that fish and plant life are unable to survive in it, hence its name. The minerals it contains include potassium, magnesium, and calcium chlorides, in addition to high levels of bromides which are very beneficial for the treatment of psoriasis, eczema, muscular pain, arthritis and rheumatism. The mineral-rich salts are renowned for their therapeutic and healing properties, as well as their ability to leave the skin clean, soft and detoxified. These versatile salts are often used to relieve tension, insomnia and to promote relaxation. Mix quantities of these salts into hand, feet and body scrubs, or dissolve them in water to create a brine solution to use as an activator in a face mask or a body wrap.

Sandalwood (powdered)

Santalum album

A wonderfully exotic natural ingredient with a delicate woody aroma, ideal for both facial and body scrubs. Make sure that the sandalwood comes from a sustainable source.

Strawberry seeds

Fragaria vesca

A delightful ingredient for a summer facial scrub. Add strawberry seeds to your recipe along with some strawberry powder (or mashed fresh strawberries), cream or yoghurt.

Dead Sea salt

Strawberry seeds

Sugar

Saccharum (cane) or Beta vulgaris (beet)
Sugar is an edible crystallized substance obtained from vegetable crops that contain lactose, sucrose and fructose. There are two types, sugar cane and sugar beet. The first is a tall tropical, fibrous grass milled for its juice which is then crystallized and refined. Sugar beet, on the other hand, is a hardy root vegetable used for centuries to feed cattle and from which a culinary sugar is obtained after various processes of juice extraction, evaporation and crystallization. Occasionally the two types of sugar are combined.

Some of the different types of sugar you can use in your scrubs are:

Granulated sugar

A medium grained sugar useful in body masks or scrubs.

Caster sugar

A finer grain of sugar that is particularly good for facial scrubs

Demerara sugar

A light brown sugar obtained from the sugar cane. Its grains are generally slightly larger than those in granulated sugar, making it an ideal ingredient for all scrubs.

Light or dark brown sugar

The colour of brown sugar comes from the addition of sugar cane molasses, thick dark syrup which remains after the sugar cane has been boiled and the sugar crystals removed. It has a fine, slightly moist texture and is a wonderful exfoliant for use in face or body scrubs. The smell is delicious, so it is unnecessary to add extra fragrance to your recipe, although ingredients such as honey, vanilla, or sweet orange oil would complement its aroma.

Demerara sugar

Light brown sugar

Dark brown sugar

Clays

For centuries mineral-rich clays have been utilized for their therapeutic properties. They are known to help improve circulation, remove toxins and impurities from the skin, tighten pores, promote healing, and leave the skin clean and soft.

Clays are renowned for their powerful absorption properties. Their ability to expand and drink up large amounts of excess oils and waste makes them beneficial to people with acne, spots, oily or problem skin. Most clays absorb toxins from the skin, however they all differ in their level of absorption, making them suitable for a range of different skin types. Each one has its own unique properties and contains different amounts of minerals and colour, depending on its source location.

Mineral-rich clays stimulate the blood circulation to the skin, exfoliate dead skin cells and rejuvenate the skin by supplying essential minerals. Using clay masks on a regular basis can improve the texture and appearance of your skin keeping it looking young and healthy.

The following are the most common cosmetic clays that can be purchased for cosmetic use. Any of these can be mixed with an activator (see page 34) and applied to the skin as a mask or body wrap. The quantities used will depend on the effect you are looking to achieve. You can also add a few tablespoons of clay to a dry or oil-based scrub to provide extra cleansing and to bring further nutrients to the skin.

Clay and henna powders on sale in Tunisia.

Note: Only use clays that have been purchased from a cosmetic supplier to ensure their purity and suitability for skincare use. Do not use clays obtained from art suppliers. Also, be careful to protect your clothing and surroundings when applying a mask as clay may stain.

Australian clays

These clays have similar properties to French clays (see page 50). They have been used by the Australian Aborigines throughout history, not only for healing, but to create decorative ceremonial markings. The Aborigines also painted themselves with clay to act as a sun block in the scorching heat of the outback. Australian clays can be purchased from cosmetic suppliers in white (kaolin), red, ivory, beige, pink, yellow, green and blue.

Bentonite clay

Bentonite montmorillonite

Formed from natural volcanic ash sediments containing over 70 minerals, including montmorillonite. Bentonite is one of the most effective and powerfully healing clays. It has extremely efficient detoxifying and healing properties and is excellent for drawing oils and toxins from the skin. It is therefore ideal for making a clay poultice, body wrap or a hair and scalp mask.

Dead Sea clay or mud

Marus limus

This clay is sourced from the depths of the Dead Sea and has exceptional therapeutic benefits. It contains many nutrients and minerals which help to detoxify the body and nourish the skin. The clay is rich in elements such as potassium, iodine and sulphur and is often used in expensive salon treatments and body wraps. It is also frequently used to ease aches and pains, as well as to treat skin conditions such as eczema, dermatitis and psoriasis. You can purchase powdered Dead Sea clay to use in dry masks and body wraps or wet Dead Sea mud which can be added to scrubs or applied straight onto the body.

Australian blue clay

Bentonite

Dead Sea mud

Fuller's earth clay

Solum fullonum

This is a naturally occurring sedimentary clay that often contains the mineral montmorillonite and a high magnesium oxide content. Fuller's earth is probably the first choice for oily skin, acne, spots and blemishes due to its superior ability to draw out oil and toxins from the skin, making it a great ingredient for facial masks. Although do not use it on sensitive or dry skin.

French clays

Montmorillonite

Montmorillonite is the name given to a group of mineral clays formed from volcanic ash, also known as French clays. These clays come from the area of Montmorillon in France where they were first discovered back in the 19th century. They contain smectite, microscopic moisture-absorbing crystals that can swell to several times their original volume. Montmorillonite clays can be green, pink or yellow depending on their mineral composition. They are extremely good at drawing impurities and toxins from the skin and for clearing up skin problems. There are many other clays from around the world with very similar properties.

French green clay

Green clay is highly absorbent and detoxifying, ideal for problem skin. It is often used to ease inflammation of the skin, to clear spots, blackheads, large pores, acne, oily and greasy skin. It is also beneficial in the repair of skin cells and tissue. Add green clay to face masks, body wraps and scrubs. However, it is not recommended for people with dry or sensitive skin.

Fuller's earth powder

Green clay

French yellow clay

High in iron oxides, yellow clay is soft and mild and does not draw out oils from the skin excessively. It is therefore well-suited to sensitive and dry skins. Yellow clay is also a useful detoxifier, cleanser and exfoliator, providing a range of nutrients to the skin.

French red clay

Its rich deep red colour comes from oxides in the rock that formed this clay. Red clay exfoliates, cleanses and detoxes the skin, leaving it both toned and rejuvenated. It is suited for people with normal to oily skin. Red clay can easily stain, so take particular care to cover up yourself and the surrounding areas when using it.

French pink clay

A mild and gentle clay containing iron oxide and silica. Pink clay stimulates the blood circulation to the skin, as well as providing gentle exfoliation and cleansing. It is therefore suitable for mature, sensitive or dry skin types.

Yellow clay

Red clay

Pink clay

Kaolin

Alternatively known as China clay or white cosmetic clay, kaolin is used in the production of ceramics, porcelain, metal casting, paint, plastics, medicine, toiletries, toothpaste and cosmetics. It forms when an element of granite, called feldspar weathers into a new mineral called kaolinite. It is a fine and gentle mineral clay high in calcium, silica, zinc and magnesium, and with natural absorbency properties, ideal for people with oily or blemished skin.

White kaolin clay is used to reduce swelling and inflammation, as well as to rejuvenate the skin. It is the most versatile, mildest and least absorbent of all the clays, gently cleansing the skin without absorbing too much oil, ideal for dry, sensitive or mature skin. Being so gentle, kaolin clay makes a good base for dry masks to which other clays can be added. Alternatively, add fruit, dairy, herb powders or seeds to kaolin clay to create dry scrubs or dry masks.

Rhassoul clay

Moroccan lava clay

An ancient clay from the Atlas Mountains of Morocco with a long history of use in cosmetics and skin-care products. Rhassoul clay is a mineral-rich, reddish brown clay packed with silica, calcium, magnesium, iron, potassium and sodium. It is frequently used to improve the skin's elasticity and to soothe areas of dry, flaky skin. With a high level of absorption this clay is most beneficial for cleansing, toning and detoxifying the skin and makes a great addition to face masks.

Kaolin

Rhassoul clay

Activators

Dry masks or scrubs need to be 'activated' or hydrated to form a paste that can easily be applied to the skin. Choose an activator which is beneficial to your skin type.

You can use any of the following ingredients to activate or hydrate your masks. If you are using water, milk or oil try warming the liquid first as the warmth will help to open and soften pores.

• Water (preferably distilled if possible)

• Milk or yoghurt

• Fruit juice

• Floral waters (such as lavender or chamomile)

• Vegetable oils (such as sweet almond, olive or borage)

• Brine (sea salts, Dead Sea salts or Epsom salts dissolved in water)

To learn more about the benefits of these ingredients read the additional information in the relevant sections.

Yoghurt

Lemon juice

Note: Adding 2–3 drops of your favourite essential oil to a face mask will give it extra therapeutic properties, as well as making it pleasant to use. See the directory of essential oils on pages 70–77 for suggestions.

Herbs and botanicals

Herbs can be purchased as cut leaves or powder. Cut leaf herbs provide extra therapeutic benefits and exfoliating properties to body scrubs. They can also be infused or macerated in oil to be used in recipes. Powdered herbs often tend to be more concentrated and can be made at home by placing dried herbs in a spice mill or coffee grinder. These powders are ideal for use in face masks, especially when combined with clays, dairy powders honey powder or fruit powders. They are also valuable contributions to herb poultices which are used to treat various ailments.

Aloe vera juice or powder
Arctium lappa
Aloe, with its antibacterial and antifungal properties, is an effective treatment for sunburn, burns and minor skin infections. It contains vitamins A, C, B complex and folic acid. Both the juice and the powder can be used in masks or scrubs.

Burdock leaf or powder
Arctium lappa
Belonging to the thistle group, both the leaf and root of the Burdock plant can be used to create scrubs and masks. The herb is frequently used as a blood purifier, as well as to minimize boils, acne, eczema, ulcers, scaly and inflamed skin.

Calendula (Marigold) petal or powder
Calendula officinalis
The orange-yellow petals of the flower are a traditional remedy for minor skin problems, such as cuts, wounds and grazes. The petals also contain beneficial skin-conditioning properties. Calendula has long been used to help inflamed skin, such as acne and sunburn, and as a herbal remedy for athlete's foot, thrush and fungal conditions. It has also been used throughout history to help prevent infection from spreading and to speed up the process of cell regeneration.

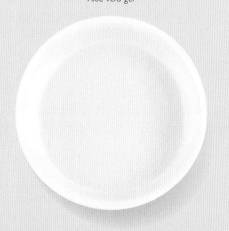

Aloe vera gel

Burdock leaf

Chamomile powder

Anthemis nobilis

Chamomile is an old favourite amongst garden herbs. This strongly aromatic white flower with a yellow centre is frequently used for its sedative and relaxing properties, and to soothe sensitive or irritated skin. Use the powder in a dry face mask, poultice or in a scrub.

Cinnamon powder

Cinnamomum zeylanicum

Reddish-brown cinnamon powder is obtained from the bark of a small evergreen tree native to the Indian subcontinent. It is often used to stimulate the circulation, to fight exhaustion and depression or to alleviate the aches and pains from rheumatism, arthritis or period pains. Use this spice sparingly – cinnamon is warming and stimulating, but can irritate the skin if too much is used. It's a fabulous ingredient for a body scrub, although not recommended for use on your face.

Comfrey leaf or root powder

Symphytum officinale

A hairy-leafed plant with light purple, cream or pink flowers, related to borage and forget-me-nots. Famously known as 'knitbone' for its ability to knit or heal the flesh, comfrey is widely used in herbal medicine for healing broken bones, sprains, cuts, wounds, bruises and for easing pain, gout, skin irritation, inflammation and haemorrhoids. This herb is a useful additive to a healing poultice.

Chamomile powder

Cinnamon powder

Comfrey root powder

Cranberry powder

Vaccinium macrocarpon
Cranberries are low-growing, woody plants, widely grown in America and Canada. The fruit is packed with vitamins and are known to have powerful antioxidant and anti-inflammatory properties.

Ginger powder

Zingiber officinale
Widely used in Chinese medicine, ginger is known to be stimulating and warming. Dried ginger is frequently used to help ease colds, stomach pain, nausea, digestion, cough, rheumatism, arthritis, muscle ache, and inflammation. As an anti-oxidant with aphrodisiac properties, ginger is a great addition to a warming scrub, although not recommended for use on the face.

Gingko biloba leaf or powder

Ginkgo biloba
Large trees with bright yellow leaves, known in China as 'silver fruit', and cultivated there for over 1,500 years. Known to be a powerful antioxidant and anti-inflammatory, ginkgo biloba is used to improve concentration, memory, circulation and to boost energy levels. Use the powder in a mask, scrub or poultice. The cut leaf can be added to scrubs.

Cranberry powder

Ginger

Gingko biloba

Ginseng powder

Panax ginseng

Originating from Asia, the name ginseng means 'the wonder of the world' or 'all-heal'. Used in Chinese herbalism for thousands of years, ginseng is most often used to combat fatigue, stress and inflammation, as well as to boost circulation and the immune system. Ginseng is also beneficial as a healthy tonic for conditioning and rejuvenating the skin or for focusing the mind.

Green tea powder

Camellia sinensis

Green tea has been used in China, Japan, India and Thailand for centuries to aid digestion, lower blood sugar and heal wounds. It is known to be a powerful antioxidant containing a wide variety of vitamins and minerals which all help to protect the skin. It also contains skin rejuvenating and healing properties beneficial for skin disease, bedsores and athlete's foot. The powder is a useful additive to a dry face mask.

Hops leaf or powder

Humulus lupulus

A well-known native British plant used as an additive in beer making. Hops are known to possess sedative properties and are valued for aiding sleep and as a traditional cure for insomnia. They can also help to ease nervous complaints, relax muscles, improve the appetite, and to soften the skin. Use hops powder in a relaxing face mask or in a scrub. Mill the spice leaves in a spice mill to obtain a powder.

Ginseng

Green tea powder

Hops

Kelp powder (seaweed)
Laminaria digitata

Kelp are large nutrient-rich sea plants (algae), commonly referred to as 'seaweed'. Abundant in amino acids, iodine and vitamins, kelp is used to tone, detox, moisturize, revitalise the skin and to boost immunity. This powdered marine plant is a great additive to spa or ocean-themed products. Kelp smells particularly strongly, so you will need to make allowances when adding fragrance to your mask or scrub.

Lavender powder
Lavandula angustifolia

This fragrant herb is legendary for its soothing, relaxing and healing properties. For centuries lavender has been used to treat burns, sunburn, muscular pains, neuralgia, rheumatism, cold sores and insect bites. It is an analgesic which helps with pain relief and has been traditionally used for its antiseptic, antibacterial and anti-inflammatory properties in the treatment of wounds, abscesses, oily skin, acne, boils and psoriasis. Mill your own powder from dried flowers to use in a scrub or dry mask.

Lemon balm
Melissa officinalis

Heart-shaped, deliciously lemon-scented leaves that can be used as a substitute for lemon in cooking. Lemon balm is one of the ingredients in Carmelite water or 'Eau de Carmes', a 17th century perfume created by Carmelite Monks which was also taken internally for nervous headaches and neuralgia. Lemon balm is also known to be effective for the nervous system, depression, memory loss, headaches, insomnia, herpes, colds, fevers and insect bites. Use the powdered herb in masks or scrubs. Cut lemon balm leaf can also be added to scrubs.

Powdered kelp

Lavender

Lemon balm

Nettle

Urtica dioica

A herbaceous flowering plant with stinging hairs. Nettle leaves are high in nutrients, such as minerals, formic acid, beta-carotene, phosphates, iron, and rich in vitamins A, C, D, and B complex, iron, potassium, manganese, calcium and nitrogen. Today, nettle is used as an astringent and a stimulating tonic, particularly for the hair. It is also used as a diuretic to stimulate the kidneys and bladder, detoxify the body, stimulate the body's immune system and to ease the symptoms of gout and arthritis. Use the powder in a poultice, mask or scrub. The cut leaf can also be added to a scrub.

Rose hip powder

Rosa canina

Rose hip powder is obtained from the fruit which is produced after the rose has flowered. Rose hips are extremely rich in vitamin C, a known antioxidant that helps to repair damaged skin. and treats scars, wrinkles and stretch marks. It also offers some protection from capillary damage, while firming and toning the skin. Rose hip powder is a great additive to a dry face mask.

Wheatgrass powder

Triticum vulgare

A vivid green powder obtained from the dried, sprouting leaves of wheatgrass. It is packed with numerous vitamins, minerals and enzymes, as well as a high proportion of chlorophyll which is known to benefit the immune system. Wheatgrass has been shown to remove toxins from the body, help acne and scars, and to restore damaged skin tissue.

Nettle

Rose hip powder

Wheatgrass powder

Honey

Bees have existed for over 50 million years and their honey has been highly valued throughout history for its antibiotic and healing properties. The Ancient Egyptians kept hives from as far back as 2400BC using the honey for embalming the dead and also eating it to promote fertility.

Beekeepers inspecting a hive.

What is honey?

Honey is a natural product produced in the hive of the honey bee. Up to 100,000 bees can live in one beehive, the majority of these are female 'worker' bees who make wax honeycomb cells in which to raise young bees and to store honey (food) for the winter. To make honey, bees fly amongst the flowers gathering a sticky sweet substance called nectar. This is mixed with a secretion of enzymes produced from the bee's mouth. The mixture is then stored in the wax honeycomb cells.

When they are full of honey, the bees cap the cells with wax. This wax is then scraped off by beekeepers in order to extract the honey. These clean wax cappings, together with some of the wax from the comb, are refined and used to produce candles and cosmetics.

Bees on a honeycomb.

Therapeutic benefits of honey

For centuries, honey has been used for medicinal purposes to nourish and heal our bodies. This golden viscous liquid is low in pH, high in simple digestible sugar and contains enzymes, pollen and trace minerals, such as zinc, calcium, magnesium, potassium, manganese, iron and selenium.

The legendary wound healing properties of honey are triggered when the enzyme glucose oxidase mixes with water or comes in contact with the skin producing hydrogen peroxide, which is known to be an anti-bacterial agent.

There are hundreds of different types of honey, the properties of which vary according to the species of flower or plant that the bees collect nectar from. Some honey is therefore more anti-bacterial than others. The most effective is Manuka honey, which has been used historically by the Maori people of New Zealand as a medicinal treatment. Manuka is highly bactericidal with powerful healing effects, so powerful in fact that it has been introduced into hospitals to fight superbugs such as MRSA.

Honey

As well as being consumed to help a multitude of ailments and for general health, honey is used to treat a wide variety of ailments such as cuts, spots, boils and ulcers. The sugars in honey acts as a humectant, drawing moisture from the air, making it highly moisturizing and beneficial for dry and sensitive skin, scars and burns. Honey is therefore a valuable addition to both scrubs and masks.

Powdered honey is also becoming widely available. It is a fabulous ingredient for dry masks and scrubs when combined with powdered herbs, milk, fruit or clays.

Tip: For a quick, antibacterial and healing cleanse, mix a little honey with water and apply to the face using cotton wool. Wash off with water before applying moisturizer.

Honey powder

Eggs and dairy

Eggs

Egg whites

These are a good base ingredient for a face mask to which other ingredients can be added, such as honey, oil, cream, or fresh yoghurt. The whites benefit your skin by narrowing your pores, reducing blackheads and acne, and giving your face a firm appearance or temporary lift. For a very simple mask, just paint egg whites onto your face and leave for 15 minutes, before washing off and applying moisturizer. Egg whites are more easily applied to the skin if they have been lightly whipped beforehand. Use the whites immediately and discard any leftovers.

Egg yolks

Applied directly to your skin, egg yolks can help ease acne, blemishes and blotches. They also moisturize, soothe and replenish the skin leaving it supple and soft. Some acne sufferers swear by simply applying egg yolk to their face, leaving it for 15 minutes, before washing it off and applying moisturizer. Use the yolk immediately and discard any leftovers.

Note: If you are allergic to any dairy products, avoid using them in your recipes.

Milk

Cow's milk, cream, sour cream, buttermilk and goat's milk all contain AHAs (Alpha Hydroxy Acids) in their lactic acid. This very effective natural acid works by dissolving the glue-like substance that binds skin cells together, thereby removing dead or flaky skin to reveal new fresh skin cells. Unlike the more abrasive facial scrubs, AHAs gently exfoliate and enhance the skin, making milk or cream-based scrubs and masks ideal for people with delicate or sensitive skin. Fresh milk can be used as an activator in masks. Alternatively, powdered milk is very effective in dry masks or scrubs.

Yoghurt

Yoghurt is a mild cleanser containing valuable AHAs. It can be used on its own as a quick and easy face mask, or combined with other ingredients, such as honey, herbs, fruit powders, clays or essential oils, for further benefits. Yoghurt is a wonderful source of protein, riboflavin, calcium and vitamin B12 and is often used for treating eczema, psoriasis, acne or skin infections. Choose natural full-fat organic yoghurt if possible. Powdered yoghurt is also a very useful addition to dry face masks.

Chocolate

Chocolate comes from the fruit of the tropical Theobroma cacao tree. The word *Theobroma* means 'food of the gods' and any chocoholic will understand why.

Cacao beans are a great source of antioxidants which protect the skin, as well as smoothing wrinkles and mature skin. They have been used medicinally for thousands of years.

Historical evidence gathered from ceramic pots shows us that Maya civilizations were using chocolate over two and a half thousand years ago. Cacao beans were first brought to Europe by Christopher Columbus on his final voyage to America in 1502. At Guanaja, he encountered a huge Mayan dugout trading canoe which contained cacao amongst its cargo. Without an interpreter, Columbus could not see why the traders valued these beans so much. He had no way of knowing that cacao beans were highly prized and used as currency, as well as to create a precious drink. It would be many years later, after his death, that the wonderful properties of these beans would be fully discovered.

Cocoa powder is made from the dark brown cocoa solids of the cacao plant, while cocoa butter comes from the same plant, but is the fatty component. Both cocoa solids and cocoa butter are used to make chocolate. Cocoa solids contain antioxidants renowned for their many health benefits.

The beans are extracted from the pods, fermented, dried, roasted, then winnowed (peeled) and ground. Over half of the dried bean contains fat (cocoa butter), the remaining solid part is cocoa (chocolate powder). The butter and powder are separated at the early stages of production for use in different manufacturing processes.

Cocoa powder is extremely high in antioxidants which fight the free radicals responsible for causing skin cell and tissue damage, as well as premature ageing. Dark chocolate contains important trace elements, minerals and vitamins including magnesium, potassium, calcium and iron which all help to 'feed the face' with nutrients. Chocolate can be used in a face mask, scrub or body wrap.

Cocoa powder

Fruit and vegetables

Fresh fruit, vegetables and juices are all easily obtainable and provide numerous benefits to the skin. They are packed full of vitamins and minerals and are fabulous, readily-available ingredients to include in your face masks.

If you use fresh produce in your products these must be used immediately or kept in the refrigerator for no more than a couple of days. If left any longer, the mixture may decay and can become harmful. Always use very ripe or over-ripe soft fruit, as fruit that is too firm will be difficult to mash and the mixture will make it hard to apply and adhere to the skin.

Powdered fruits are spray-dried from fresh fruit, in order to preserve valuable vitamins and minerals. They are becoming widely available and provide excellent therapeutic properties to your dry face masks and scrubs. If stored correctly, most powdered fruits have a shelf life of around 18 months, but its always best to ask the supplier when purchasing them. In their powdered form, fruit has a mild fruity scent, but when hydrated with a liquid activator the full wonderful fruity aroma is let loose – delicious! Some of the top salons and spas offer tropical fruit masks and body wraps made from powdered fruits – if you can't afford a trip to the Caribbean, this is a great alternative!

Making a fresh face mask with strawberries is a great way to use up any leftover and overripe produce.

Powdered and fresh banana

Apple

Pyrus malus

Apple pulp, juice or powder contains a mild fruit acid which helps to moisturize, rejuvenate and refine your skin. A great ingredient for toning tired and stressed skin or dry, mature skin.

Apricot

Prunus armeniaca

Apricot pulp, juice or powder is a rich source of vitamin A, vitamin C, potassium, iron, phosphorus, and calcium, all wonderful properties to regenerate, soothe, nourish and moisturize dry or mature skin. Apricot can also help to protect the skin and to remove impurities.

Avocado

Persea gratissima

Avocado has to be the queen of the fruits for the skin, as well as a fantastic moisturizer. It is extremely rich in nutrients and highly beneficial for dry skin. Vitamin A helps to restore a youthful appearance, while vitamin E protects and repairs the skin after sun damage or pollution. For a quick mask, simply mash some very ripe avocado, apply to the skin, rinse and moisturize.

Banana

Musa sapientum

Banana pulp and powder are rich in potassium and vitamin A, perfect for people with sensitive or dry skin. Simply mash an over-ripe banana and apply it to your face as a moisturizing face mask.

Carrots

Daucus carota

Cooked, mashed carrots and carrot juice both contain high levels of beta carotene which helps to combat dry skin and wrinkles. Mashed carrots can also be used to treat eczema, wounds, burns, acne, spots, sunburn, wrinkles, and stretch marks.

Cucumber

Cucumis sativus

Cucumber pulp or powder are both well-known tonics for cooling and soothing the skin. Place a fresh slice of cucumber over each eye after applying a face mask to soften, hydrate and refresh the skin. Cucumber can also be used to help treat spots, blackheads, oily skin, wrinkles, rosacea, dermatitis or to relieve sunburn.

Grapefruit

Citrus grandis

Grapefruit juice, pulp or powder has a detoxing and toning effect on the skin. It is rich in antioxidants and its cleansing properties are useful for treating acne and spotty skin.

Guava

Psidium guajava

Guava pulp and powder are prized for toning and tightening the skin, as well as its anti-ageing properties. High in anti-oxidants, potassium, and vitamins A, B and C, Guava helps to detoxify the skin giving it a youthful glow.

Kiwi

Actinidia chinensis

Kiwi pulp or powder is packed with the antioxidants vitamins C and E. It is known to stimulate collagen and to tighten the pores in your skin.

Lemon

Citrus medica limonum

Rich in vitamin C, lemon is renowned for its numerous skin-enhancing properties. The fruit acid exfoliates dead skin cells, to reveal new healthy skin, while its astringent properties make it excellent for oily skin and acne. Lemon juice, pulp or powder are all easily available.

Mango

Mangifera indica

Mango juice, pulp and powder are all extremely high in vitamins A, C and beta-carotene. Mango is used in skin-care preparations to prevent wrinkles, restore the skin's elasticity, and to moisturize dry skin.

Orange/mandarin/tangerine

Citrus dulcis/Citrus nobilis/Citrus tangerina

The juice of all three contain high levels of vitamin C, an important antioxidant which helps to protect the skin against damage and premature ageing. Add to cocoa powder for a fantastic chocolate-orange face mask to create a glowing complexion and a delicious aroma.

Papaya

Carica papaya

Papaya (or pawpaw), whether juice, pulp or powder, is another fruit packed with vitamins. It is often used to help acne and spots, large pores, dry flaky skin, and wrinkles. It is also excellent for removing dead skin cells. To exfoliate and brighten your skin, simply rub fresh papaya into your skin and wash off.

Peach

Prunus persica

Peach pulp or powder contains the vitamins C and V, potassium, phosphorus, and magnesium. It has mild astringent properties which makes it ideal for revitalizing tired, dry and dull skin.

Pineapple

Ananas sativus

Pineapple juice, pulp and powder are all full of powerful enzymes which cleanse, invigorate and exfoliate the skin. Rich in potassium, calcium, and vitamin C, pineapple can help with free-radical damage, reducing the appearance of fine lines and age spots, to leave your skin soft, supple and glowing.

Potato

Solanum tuberosum

Raw potato contains minerals, starches and proteins. When moistened with water, slices of potato can be very beneficial for easing skin irritation. Simply cut the potato into slices, run under a warm tap and apply to your skin. If you have puffy eyes, place a slice of potato onto your closed eyelid for five to ten minutes to reduce the inflammation and puffiness.

Strawberries

Fragaria vesca

Strawberry pulp and powder are both fantastic ingredients to include in face masks. They smell divine and are rich in vitamin C which helps with anti-ageing, and can help to remove impurities, as well as reducing redness and swelling. They contain mild fruit acids which help to exfoliate dead cells, leaving your skin cleansed, refreshed and bright.

Tomatoes

Solanum lycopersicum

Tomatoes are rich in vitamins, minerals, iron and potassium. They have an astringent effect, helping to remove excess oil and to shrink and refine enlarged pores. They are also used to eradicate acne, spots, blackheads, rashes and blemishes. Simply slice a tomato in two, rub one half onto your face, rinse, then moisturize to leave your skin looking bright and healthy.

Watermelon

Citrullus lanatus

Watermelon, both pulp and powder, is known for its anti-inflammatory, detoxifying and moisturizing properties. Rich in potassium and vitamin C it is an antioxidant that helps to rejuvenate and detoxify the skin, as well as prevent outbreaks of acne and spots.

Essential oils

Essential oils are the spirit, personality or essence of an aromatic plant. They are the fragrant, natural volatile liquids found in plants, leaves, fruit, seeds, roots, wood, resin, rum, grasses and flowers. These oils are known to have many different therapeutic benefits and have been used for centuries for their antiseptic, anti-viral, anti-fungal and anti-bacterial properties. They are also widely used in the practice of aromatherapy to help ease a multitude of complaints and conditions.

Aromatherapy

Aromatherapy is a form of complementary, holistic practice of caring for the body via inhalation or topical application of aromatic plant oils. These essential oils are applied in several ways including massage, inhalation, vaporisation, compresses, bath and skincare products to ease common ailments, aid relaxation, and to improve physical, mental and emotional health.

A particular smell can instantly trigger distinctive memories and associations from our past; a special relative, childhood trip, or memories of places from the past. Aromas can also trigger changes in our moods; a stroll in a fragrant rose garden, for example, can lift and calm your spirits, whilst a walk down a dirty street may have the opposite effect. The aroma of essential oils affects our mood in the same way; simply by breathing in the floral aroma of lavender we feel relaxed, calm and de-stressed, whereas the scent of lemons awakens our senses, invigorates and refreshes the mind.

The term 'aromathérapie' was created in the 1920s by a French Chemist, René-Maurice Gattefossé. It literally means a therapy using aromas. Gattefossé is reputed to have discovered the healing and antiseptic properties of essential oils when he burned his arm and cooled it down with lavender oil, the substance closest to hand. The pain relief and speedy healing that followed prompted him to spend his life researching the subject. In 1964 Dr Jean Valnet, carried out further research into these healing properties of oils on wounded soldiers and published his well-known aromatherapists' bible *The Practice of Aromatherapy*. Aromatherapy has become one of the most and popular complementary therapies.

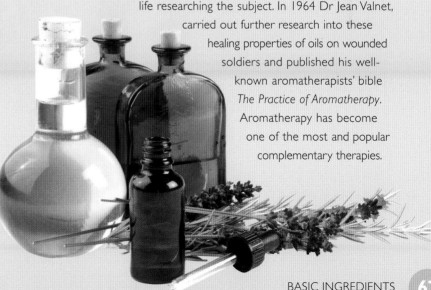

Safety

Essential oils should never be used neat or applied directly to the skin – always use a carrier oil. They are very potent and only a small amount is used in cosmetics; we therefore advise that the amounts stated in the recipes are not exceeded. Some essential oils should not be used over certain percentages, so care should be taken to read the information provided on each essential oil before making your own recipes. If you suffer from allergies, we also advise doing a skin test patch beforehand.

These oils should not be taken internally and must be kept away from young children and animals. If they are accidentally swallowed, obtain medical help immediately. If any of the oils get into the eye area, irrigate with water immediately, and if symptoms persist seek medical advice.

Essential oils from some citrus fruits – grapefruit, bergamot, orange, lemon, petitgrain and lime – are phototoxic and can react with sunlight, so avoid direct exposure from the sun for approximately 12 hours after use.

Although essential oils have been historically used to ease various medical conditions, aromatherapy is a complementary therapy and should in no way be a substitute for medical advice.

Most essential oils should be avoided by children under the age of seven; the exceptions to this are lavender, geranium, chamomile, mandarin, and yarrow, and these should be used at no more than 0.5%. The essential oils in recipes can always be adapted for use with young children or a synthetic fragrance oil can be used instead.

Safety measures

Seek advice from a qualified practitioner or medical adviser if you:

- have a known medical condition, such as high blood pressure or epilepsy
- are receiving any psychiatric or medical treatment
- are taking medication
- are pregnant or breast-feeding
- wish to treat young children

Lavender is a popular and widely available essential oil, which is safe to use for most, even young children.

Storage

Essential oils should be stored in dark coloured glass jars or bottles in a cool environment. Many oils can last for years if stored in this way, however citrus oils will generally lose their properties approximately one year after purchase. As with perfumes, exposure to oxygen will quickly degrade essential oils, so make sure that there is as little space between the surface of the oil and the top of the bottle as possible.

These oils can also damage clothing and wooden surfaces, so cover yourself and any surfaces before using them.

How much essential oil?

Face masks:
Add 2–3 drops of essential oil to each face mask application, when adding your activator.

Body wraps:
Add up to 1% of essential oils to the mixture, when combining with an activator. As a guide, for a whole body wrap use approximately ¼–½ teaspoon (1.25–2.5ml or 25–50 drops).

Scrubs:
You can add up to 3% of essential oil. For example, 3ml (60 drops) to 3½oz (100g) of scrub. Although for peppermint, black pepper or tea tree oil no more than1% should be added to the scrub.

Selected essential oils

There are numerous essential oils to choose from, too many to list in this book. On the following pages I have selected some of the most useful oils to have at hand with brief descriptions of each. This is followed by a simple chart on page 77, clearly showing their main therapeutic benefits.

Black pepper

Piper nigrum

Principal use: Warming, easing muscle pain.

Fragrance: Fresh, warm, sharp, spicy dry-woody smell.

Origins: One of the oldest known spices, used for thousands of years to season and preserve food, as well as a form of currency. Black pepper was an expensive commodity originating from India and Indonesia and traded throughout the world. The word 'Pep', as in 'Pep Talk' or 'Pep you up', comes from the word pepper inspired by its energy, vigour and spirit. The essential oil is produced by steam distillation of dried, crushed, slightly under ripe fruits.

Therapeutic benefits: The profoundly warming and stimulating properties of black pepper increase the circulation to the skin, making it a good choice for people who feel the cold, have cold hands and feet, suffer from chilblains, or for those who are feeling weak and lacking in energy. Its anti-microbial properties make pepper especially beneficial for people suffering from colds, flu or viruses. It is also used as an analgesic for the treatment of rheumatism, tired aching limbs and muscular aches or stiffness. This aromatic oil can also help with bruising, cellulite, muscle tone, digestion, constipation, problems with the kidneys, anaemia and the spleen, loss of appetite and flatulence. Black pepper is also reputed to have aphrodisiac properties.

Blends with: sandalwood, frankincense, juniper, rosemary, cardamom, fennel, cedarwood, ginger, bergamot, neroli, clary sage, clove, coriander, fennel, geranium, grapefruit, lavender, lemon, lime, mandarin, sage and ylang-ylang.

Safety: Not recommended in concentrations of more than 1%.

Chamomile (Roman)

Anthemis nobilis

Principal use: Relieving inflammation and stress.

Fragrance: Refreshing, sweet, herbaceous, apple-like, fresh scent.

Origins: Roman chamomile is native to southern and western Europe, where it has been used for centuries for its healing properties. When walked upon, chamomile releases its essential oils creating a wonderfully scented aroma. Chamomile oil is steam distilled from the flowers.

Therapeutic benefits: As one of the most gentle essential oils, chamomile is frequently used in many baby and children's products, especially those for easing colic or teething troubles. This soothing and calming oil is also known to have a sedative effect useful for nervous digestion problems, indigestion, colic and diarrhoea. It has been used for thousands of years as a muscle relaxant and for treating abdominal pain or spasms, arthritis, back pain, rheumatism, neuralgia, menstrual cramps, migraine, inflammation, PMS, asthma and hayfever. It is also effective on skin irritations and complaints, such as bites, stings, acne, eczema, dermatitis, rashes and wounds, as well as post-natal depression, insomnia, stress, addictions or anorexia.

Blends with: Clary sage, bergamot, lavender, lemon, geranium, jasmine, tea tree, grapefruit, lemon, ylang-ylang, marjoram and rose geranium.

Eucalyptus

Eucalyptus globulus

Principal use: Respiratory and aching muscles.

Fragrance: Strong medicinal, sharp, fresh, camphoraceous smell with slight woody undertones.

Origins: Also known as the Blue Gum tree, the plant has been used historically as a medicinal herb in Australia by the Aborigines. The essential oil is obtained by steam distillation of fresh or partially dried leaves and young twigs.

Therapeutic benefits: Soothing and calming, cooling and deodorizing, eucalyptus is used for fevers, malaria, pneumonia, colds, flu, measles, chicken pox, bronchitis, asthma, sinusitis, throat infections and catarrh. With a stimulating effect on the mind, it can also help with headaches and concentration. As an analgesic it is used to ease insect bites, muscular aches and pains, rheumatoid arthritis, stiffness, sprains, sports injuries, as well as poor circulation. With antibacterial and antifungal properties, eucalyptus oil is used In skincare to heal ulcers, wounds, cystitis, herpes, skin eruptions, spots, congested skin, athlete's foot, the urinary tract and genital infections.

Blends with: Cypress, lavender, marjoram, lemongrass, thyme, tea tree, lemon and pine.

Safety: This oil must not be swallowed as it is toxic if taken internally. Keep away from children and pets.

Frankincense

Boswellia carterii

Principal use: Mature skin and meditation.

Fragrance: Fresh top note with sweet, woody, resinous undertones.

Origins: Also known as *olibanum* (meaning 'oil from Lebanon'), frankincense is a natural oleo-gum resin obtained from the bark of the Boswellia tree. These trees are native to the mountainous areas of western India, southern Arabia and north-east Africa. Incisions are made into the bark of uncultivated trees to allow a milky-white substance to seep out, this hardens into amber resin, crystal tears which are graded according to their quality. The oil is then produced by steam to distill the resin. Frankincense was used by many ancient civilisations, as far back as the ancient Egyptians. The name is derived from the French word *franc* which means pure, and the Latin *incensum*, meaning smoke. It was for this 'pure smoke' that the oil was coveted in ancient times, used widely in religious ceremonies and for fumigation of the sick.

Therapeutic benefits: The ancient Egyptians would use frankincense in the mummifying process, so it is no surprise that this aromatic oil is used in aromatherapy for rejuvenating and toning dry, mature skin, minimize wrinkles and treating scars, wounds and ulcers. With its anti-inflammatory and astringent properties, frankincense can be used to treat respiratory conditions such as asthma, laryngitis, bronchitis, catarrh and mucus conditions. By adding a few drops to a face mask, for example, it can help clear the lungs and ease the symptoms of colds and coughs, slow down breathing and calm the mind making it ideal for meditation or for relieving stress, anxiety and tension.

Blends with: Basil, neroli, pine, sandalwood, myrrh, vetiver, cedarwood, orange, sandalwood, lavender, rose geranium, bergamot and lemon.

Ginger

Zingiber officinale

Principal use: Circulation, colds and flu.

Fragrance: Hot, dry, pungent and musty, with a lingering spicy sweetness.

Origins: Ginger has been used as a culinary spice and as a remedy for malaria, rheumatism and toothache in its native India since very early times. Ginger was taken along the spice route to Europe where it was used by the Greeks and Romans.

Therapeutic benefits: Warming, heating and toning, ginger is a well-known remedy for colds, flu, fevers, lungs, respiratory complaints, and poor circulation. With its analgesic properties ginger can help to ease muscular pain and aches, rheumatic pain, arthritis, chillblains, cold feet, diminish bruises, and boost the immune system. Ginger root is has been traditionally used in Chinese medicine for soothing digestion, as well as nausea, travel or morning sickness, stomach-ache, and diarrhoea, as well as stimulating the heart. It is also known to be an aphrodisiac.

Blends with: All citrus and spicy oils, in particular bergamot, black pepper, frankincense, neroli, rose geranium, sandalwood, vetiver, juniper, ylang ylang and cedarwood.

Safety: This oil may irritate sensitive skins.

Grapefruit

Citrus grandis

Principal use: Detoxing and reviving.

Fragrance: Fresh, green, zesty, sweet, citrus smell.

Origins: The grapefruit is a citrus hybrid from a sweet orange and a pomelo, which is believed to have originated from the West Indies. The name alludes to the grape-like clusters of fruit growing on the tree. It is now grown extensively in America, China, South Africa and Israel. The essential oil is obtained by expressing the grapefruit peel.

Therapeutic benefits: Uplifting and revitalizing, grapefruit oil is known to be beneficial for lifting the spirits and for treating stress, depression and nervous exhaustion. Anyone who is lethargic and lacking in energy, suffering from jet lag, overindulgence or a hangover may be revived and re-energized by using grapefruit oil. The oil also stimulates the lymphatic system and is a very useful for people with constipation, digestive, liver and kidney problems. Grapefruit also helps to combat obesity, water retention, cellulite, muscle fatigue and stiffness. Its high vitamin C content makes it a very useful oil if you are suffering from a cold or a weakened immune system. Its mildly astringent properties can also help minimize oily skin, spots and acne and tone the skin.

Blends with: Bergamot, palmarosa, geranium, frankincense, eucalyptus and pine.

Safety: This oil is mildly phototoxic. Avoid sunlight for 12 hours after use, as the oil can react with the sunlight and irritate the skin.

Lavender

Lavandula angustifolia

Principal use: Healing and relaxing.

Fragrance: Fresh, light, soft, sweet floral.

Origins: Lavender oil is native to the Mediterranean and has been grown extensively for many years in the Provence region of France. It is also grown in England, Italy, Morocco, Africa and India. Lavender grown at high altitudes is considered to be of the best quality. The Romans would use lavender to bathe in, indeed the name is derived from the Roman word *lavare* meaning to bath or to wash. It was also used to treat sores and wounds and as a disinfectant in hospitals during the First World War. Although the leaves are very aromatic, it is the lavender flower that is distilled to produce the essential oil. Widely used in perfumery, lavender blends well with many other essential oils.

Therapeutic benefits: Lavender is an ideal oil to keep in your first aid kit; it is an extremely useful and versatile oil, and the most widely used due to its numerous therapeutic benefits. Not only is it known to help reduce swelling, heal wounds, burns, stings, bites and shock, it is also a beneficial oil to have on hand for its pain-killing and stress-relieving properties. Lavender has been used throughout the ages to ease stress, nervous tension, acne, insomnia, neuralgia, eczema, psoriasis, thrush, psoriasis, dermatitis, rosacae and scarring. When applied to the temples, lavender oil soothes headaches and migraines, aids sleep and relaxation, and is a great addition to a face mask. Lavender water also makes a useful activator for a face mask or body wrap.

Blends with: All oils.

Lemon

Citrus medica limonum

Principal use: Immune system, antiseptic.

Fragrance: Fresh, sweet, green, citrus smell.

Origins: The lemon tree originated in India and China and was brought to Europe and the Middle East in the 12th century. The oil is extracted from the fresh fruit peel by cold expression.

Therapeutic benefits: The astringent properties of lemon are effective at clearing congested and oily skin, thereby helping to diminish abscesses, boils, acne, spots and minor wounds. It also helps to reduce the acidity in the body which can assist with digestion, arthritis, rheumatism and gout. Lemon oil has been used historically to boost the immune system, to treat colds and flu, and for helping with lethargy and fatigue. It also lifts the spirits, stimulates the mind and boosts concentration, so it is a great for taking when sitting exams or if experiencing jet lag. Lemon oil is also used in aromatherapy to help ease depression, stress, high blood pressure, varicose veins and circulation, as well as a tonic for aiding lymphatic drainage, obesity and cellulite.

Blends with: Lavender, rose geranium, sandalwood, benzoin, eucalyptus, fennel, juniper and neroli.

Safety: This oil is phototoxic, so avoid sunlight for 12 hours after use. It may also cause sensitization.

Mandarin

Citrus nobilis

Principal use: Toning and digestion.

Fragrance: Very sweet, rich, tangy, zesty-floral scent.

Origins: Native to China and the Far East, the mandarin orange was a traditional offering to the Chinese mandarins which is where the name is believed to have originated. The oil is machine expressed from the peel of the ripe fruit.

Therapeutic benefits: Throughout history, this oil has been used to clear congested, oily skin and acne, to smooth stretch marks and to increase circulation. Its qualities mean that it can help to regulate the metabolism and aid the breakdown of fats, thereby reducing fluid retention, obesity and cellulite. It is also great for toning the skin after losing weight, easing digestion, stomach cramps, nervous indigestion, flatulence, diarrhoea and constipation. The soothing and sedative properties of mandarin make it beneficial for use with people with nervous disorders, stress and insomnia. It is a very gentle and relaxing oil used in aromatherapy to calm hyperactive children and in treating the elderly.

Blends with: Chamomile, lavender, frankincense, bergamot, clary sage, juniper, lavender, nutmeg and neroli.

Patchouli

Pogostemon cablin

Principal use: Depression and scars.

Fragrance: Aromatic, woody and musky with spicy, musty, and earthy-sweet undertones.

Origins: Native to the tropical regions of Asia, this oil has been used historically for incense and perfume, as well as to repel insects and moths. The oil is extracted by steam distillation of the leaves.

Therapeutic benefits: This is a helpful oil for alleviating anxiety, depression, nervous strain, and other stress-related problems with its soothing and calming effect. It is often used in skincare to help reduce the appearance of scars, stretch marks, acne and as a skin conditioner for dry, cracked or ageing skin. As an antiseptic and anti-inflammatory it is also beneficial for treating eczema, sores, skin inflammations and may help to reduce the appearance of cellulite. It is anti-bacterial, an insecticide and fungicide and is therefore useful for skin and fungal infections such as impetigo and athlete's foot. It has also traditionally been used as an aphrodisiac.

Blends with: Bergamot, lavender, rose geranium, chamomile, clary sage, cedarwood and myrrh.

Peppermint

Mentha piperita

Principal use: Revitalizing and digestion.

Fragrance: Strong, fresh, minty with sweet undertones.

Origins: This fragrant herb has a long history of medicinal use, with archaeological evidence placing its use at least as far back as 10,000 years ago. The oil is produced by steam-distillation of the herb.

Therapeutic benefits: Peppermint oil is refreshing, cooling and revitalizing, a useful and powerful oil with which to aid concentration or when suffering from mental fatigue, headaches or migraines. One of its primary uses is in the treatment of digestive disorders such as nausea, morning sickness, travel sickness, stomach cramps, irritable bowel syndrome, indigestion, flatulence and hiccups. Peppermint is also used as an analgesic to relieve pain from muscle ache, lumbago, neuralgia, bruises, joint aches and insect bites and as a decongestant to treat coughs, colds and flu, bronchitis, sinusitis and asthma. A few drops of peppermint oil in a body scrub makes a very invigorating and refreshing treatment to awaken the senses and to increase the circulation.

Blends with: Rosemary, black pepper, eucalyptus, lavender, marjoram, ginger and lemon.

Safety: This oil can occasionally be sensitizing. Not recommended in concentrations of more than 1%.

Rose geranium

Pelargonium graveolens and Pelargonium rosa

Principal use: Skin problems, soothing.

Fragrance: Fresh, crisp, sweet rosy scent.

Origins: Geranium plants initially came from South Africa, Madagascar, Egypt and Morocco. There are several different types of geranium essential oil, rose geranium is just one of them. The plants are now grown extensively for use in the perfume industry. The foliage is distilled to make the essential oil which is often used as a substitute for rose oil.

Therapeutic benefits: Rose geranium is an anti-depressant, anti-septic and anti-inflammatory, balancing the skin by regulating the secretion of sebum (the skin's natural oil) making it useful for both dry and oily skin. With excellent wound healing properties, rose geranium oil has been used historically to clear spots, scars, acne, burns, bruises and eczema. It is also known to be beneficial in the treatment of haemorrhoids, gall stones, jaundice, ulcers, wounds, lice and ringworm. It is also used to ease stress, tension, anxiety, depression, PMT, hormonal problems and heavy periods, as well as relieving the pain from neuralgia, muscle ache or shingles. As a diuretic, rose geranium can help to stimulate the lymphatic system which eliminates toxins, fluid retention and cellulite. Gastroenteritis, diarrhoea or stomach aches can benefit from the soothing and cooling properties of rose geranium oil. Pain from neuralgia, muscle ache or shingles may be relieved by using this oil.

Blends with: Basil, bergamot, cedarwood, grapefruit, rosemary, clary sage, lavender, jasmine, lemon, orange, neroli and lime.

Rosemary

Rosmarinus officinalis

Principal use: Aching muscles and circulation problems.

Fragrance: Strong, fresh, herbaceous, camphoraceous scent.

Origins: Rosemary is a native of the Mediterranean region where it still grows in abundance. For thousands of years rosemary has been used as a sacred herb to drive away evil spirits and to heal the sick. The oil is steam distilled from the flowers, leaves and twigs of the plant.

Therapeutic benefits: Rosemary oil is an analgesic (pain reliever) and is reported to be beneficial for treating arthritis, rheumatism, muscular aches and pains, sprains, painful periods, as well as overworked muscles. The oil is said to increase the circulation of the blood to the nervous system and the brain, thereby boosting concentration and easing headaches and migraines, as well as stimulating the mind and memory. The oil is often recommended as a tonic for the liver and gallbladder, for colds and flu, digestion, low blood pressure, palpitations, and circulation problems. Rosemary is also a traditional remedy for painful digestion, colic, gallbladder infection, flatulence, diarrhoea, colitis and for liver problems. The oil is also used extensively in hair products; a few drops of rosemary essential oil added to a hair mask may help to strengthen the scalp, ease alopecia, dandruff, scabies or lice, and encourage new hair growth.

Blends with: Cedarwood, geranium, bergamot, basil, lavender, lemongrass and peppermint.

Safety: This oil is not recommended for people with high blood pressure or if you are pregnant.

Tea tree

Melaleuca alternifolia

Principal use: Antibacterial and anti-infectious.

Fragrance: Fresh, strong, spicy, pungent camphoraceous.

Origins: Tea tree is native to New South Wales, Australia, and has been used for thousands of years by the Aborigines as an antiseptic and for a variety of other medicinal purposes. Captain Cook is said to have named the plant back in the 18th century when the leaves were used to make tea as a remedy for scurvy. The oil is distilled from the leaves and twigs.

Therapeutic benefits: Tea tree essential oil has been used for centuries to boost the immune system, to help the body fight off infections, for shock, and for lifting the spirits. This oil can also be useful for easing aching muscles, asthma, bronchitis, coughs, sinusitis, whooping cough, abscesses, tuberculosis, acne, burns, oily skin, athlete's foot, blisters, callous, cuts, boils, warts, cold sores, blemishes, insect stings and bites. Tea tree also has potent anti-viral, antibacterial, anti-fungal and anti-microbial properties, useful for relieving colds, viruses, skin infections, vaginal thrush, genital infections, cystitis or herpes.

Blends with: Clove, lavender, eucalyptus, rosemary, lemon pine and thyme.

Safety: Some people are sensitive to this oil. It is not recommended in concentrations of more than 1%.

Essential oil therapeutic benefits chart

	Black Pepper	Chamomile	Eucalyptus	Frankincense	Ginger	Grapefruit	Lavender	Lemon	Mandarin	Patchouli	Peppermint	Rose geranium	Rosemary	Tea tree
Acne		●	●	●		●	●	●	●	●		●		●
Antibacterial		●	●				●	●		●		●	●	●
Anti-fungal			●				●			●				●
Antiseptic	●	●	●	●	●	●	●	●		●		●	●	●
Anti-inflammatory		●	●	●			●					●		
Cellulite	●		●			●		●	●	●		●	●	
Circulation	●		●	●				●	●		●		●	
Concentration			●	●							●		●	
Coughs			●	●	●						●		●	●
Cuts/wounds			●	●			●	●		●				●
Depression		●				●	●	●		●	●	●	●	
Detoxing	●					●	●					●		
Digestion	●				●	●	●		●		●		●	
Dry skin				●						●		●		
Eczema		●					●			●		●		
Exhaustion/fatigue	●				●			●			●		●	
Headaches		●				●	●	●			●		●	
Healing		●	●	●			●	●		●		●		●
Insomnia		●	●				●					●		
Muscle pain	●	●	●			●	●				●	●	●	●
Oily skin						●		●	●	●		●		●
Psoriasis		●					●			●		●		
Rheumatism	●	●	●	●			●				●		●	
Skin problems		●	●	●			●			●		●		●
Scars/stretch marks				●			●		●			●		
Stress		●		●	●	●	●	●	●	●	●	●		

Fixed vegetable oils

You will often find the words 'fixed oils' written on a supplier's list. These are oils that do not evaporate and are not soluble in water. They are highly emollient and are therefore often used as carrier oils for massage or body scrubs. The difference between 'fixed' and 'essential oils' is that essential oils are volatile, they will evaporate and are soluble in water. Essential oils are highly fragrant and potent and must be mixed with 'fixed' oils so that they can be safely applied to the skin.

Fixed oils are obtained from the abundance of seeds, nuts and kernels of plants from all over the world. Many of these are high in antioxidants, which help combat the destructive effects of free radicals on the skin. Others are known for their therapeutic and skin-renewal benefits and used to treat skin conditions such as eczema and psoriasis, or to help reduce the appearance of scars and wrinkles. Antimicrobial studies of natural oils have shown that some oils can even reduce the amount of bacteria.

Vegetable oils are traditionally obtained by pressing, crushing and often refining the seeds, nuts and kernels of plants and are liquid at room temperature. The traditional and natural 'cold-pressed' method of oil extraction yields the best quality oil from seeds, leaving it as close as possible to its natural state. The oil is literally squeezed or pressed out of the seeds and then filtered to remove the sediment or husks. These essential parts of the plants' system contain high levels of different fatty acids, vitamins and minerals with antioxidant, anti-inflammatory and moisturizing properties.

Macerated oils

Herbs are macerated (infused) in a carrier oil which releases the plant's therapeutic volatile properties into the oil. Macerated oils can be applied directly to the skin or used to create your scrubs and masks.

Base or 'carrier' oils

Certain oils are particularly useful as the emollient base in your body scrubs. The more expensive, precious, macerated or infused oils can be added to these for their therapeutic benefits. They are highly beneficial in their own right, as they are easily applied to the skin and are quickly absorbed.

Caution: Those with nut allergies should check the suitability of nut oils before using them in recipes.

Apricots

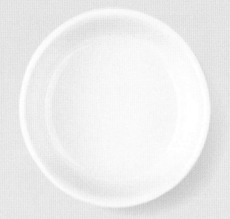

Grapeseed oil

Hemp

Apricot kernel oil

Prunus armeniaca

Similar to sweet almond or peach oil, as this light oil is pressed from the kernel of the apricot fruit. High in essential fatty acids, linoleic and oleic acids, it is said to be beneficial and nourishing to sensitive, dehydrated and mature skin. Apricot kernel oil is beneficial for fine lines, delicate and sensitive areas. This oil is easily absorbed into the skin and makes a good base oil.

Grapeseed oil

Vitis vinifera

A bi-product of the wine-making industry, grapeseed oil is made from the seeds of grapes. It is easily absorbed into the skin and used in the cosmetics industry to support cell membranes, reduce the appearance of stretch marks, and to help repair damaged skin tissue. This oil is easily absorbed into the skin and makes a good base oil.

Hempseed oil

Cannabis sativa

Extracted from the seeds of the hemp plant which is high in unsaturated fatty acids including palmitoleic, oleic, linoleic and gamma-linolenic acid (GLA). This oil is widely used in cosmetics due to the unique balance of its essential fatty acids (EFAs) which complements the proportions of EFAs required by the human body. Hempseed oil also helps to ease inflammation and the symptoms of eczema and psoriasis.

Corn oil

Zea mays

Corn oil is extracted from the germ of the seeds. It is high in vitamin E and essential fatty acids and makes an inexpensive base oil for scrubs.

Jojoba

Olive

Sunflower seeds

Jojoba oil

Simmondsia chinensis

A native shrub from the deserts of Arizona, California and Mexico, jojoba oil is actually a liquid wax obtained from the seeds. This oil is similar to our own skin's sebum – the skin's natural oil – making it readily absorbed and ideal for use in face masks or hair-care products. Rich in proteins and minerals, jojoba helps soothe eczema, psoriasis, and dry or sensitive skin. Jojoba oil will go solid if refrigerated so leave for a few hours at room temperature before use if it has been stored in a refrigerator.

Olive oil

Olea europaea

Grown mainly in the Mediterranean, olive oil is a green to golden brown colour depending on the quality. It is a complex compound of fatty acids, high in oleic acid, vitamins A, K, E (a natural antioxidant), and many other important vitamins and minerals.
Olive oil is reported to ease burns, inflammation, arthritis, wounds, and dry skin. It also makes a nourishing base oil.

Peach kernel oil

Prunus persica

This oil is easily absorbed into the skin making it a good base oil. Its properties are very similar to sweet almond oil.

Sunflower oil

Helianthus annuus

Produced from the seeds of the well -known flower, this oil is packed with vitamins A, D and E, minerals, lecithin and essential fatty acids, and is ideal for soothing mature, dry, damaged or sensitive skin. This oil is easily absorbed into the skin and makes a good oil base.

Sweet almond oil

Prunus dulcis

Pressed from the kernels of the sweet almond fruit and prized since ancient times. Sweet almond oil contains the vitamins A, B1, B2 and B6 and E. It is a wonderful emollient used to nourish, protect and condition the skin, calm skin irritation, and to soften dry areas. Its versatility makes it a fabulous base oil.

Precious and therapeutic oils

The following more precious or macerated oils can be added toyour scrubs, masks and wraps for extra therapeutic benefits.

Many of these oils are particularly good for the face or as an activator in face masks.

Argan oil

Argania spinosa

The kernels of the ancient argan tree are hand-pressed to produce this oil. Argan oil contains fatty acids and vitamin E, a powerful antioxidant, that nourishes and protects the skin, promotes its elasticity and reduces scars and wrinkles.

Arnica oil

Arnica montana

This macerated oil is ideal for use as a muscle rub or bath oil after sport and for easing arthritis, rheumatism, bruises, swellings, pulled muscles, backache, sore joints, muscle pain, sore ligaments or cartilage. Do not use on broken skin.

Avocado oil

Persea gratissima

Avocado oil is easily absorbed into the skin and frequently used for sun-damaged or dehydrated skin, eczema or psoriasis. It is highly emollient and moisturizing, ideal for rejuvenating mature skin.

Blackcurrant seed oil

Ribes nigrum

This vitamin-rich oil is high in gamma-linolenic acid, an essential fatty acid that is needed, but not produced by the body. It is a great addition to face preparations.

Borage oil

Borago officinalis

This oil is obtained from the seeds of the borage plant. It contains the highest amount of gamma linolenic acid and is used for skin disorders such as psoriasis, inflammation, arthritis, eczema and for replenishing dry skin.

Borage oil

Calendula (Marigold) oil

Calendula officinalis

The orange-yellow petals of this flower are a traditional remedy for minor skin problems, such as cuts, wounds and grazes. Calendula is a macerated herb oil which also provides beneficial skin-conditioning properties. It has long been used to help inflamed skin such as acne and sunburn and as a herbal remedy for athlete's foot, thrush and fungal conditions. It has also been used to prevent infection from spreading and to speed up cell regeneration.

Carrot tissue oil

Evening primrose

Hazelnuts growing

Carrot tissue oil

Daucus carota

A golden yellow/orange oil extracted from the flesh of carrots. Very rich in beta carotene and vitamins, carrot tissue oil is a powerful antioxidant extremely useful for cell regeneration and for those with dry, cracked or mature skin. The beta carotene in this oil makes this a very strongly coloured orange oil, so use it carefully as it can stain. Carrot tissue is a macerated oil.

Castor oil

Ricinus communis

Obtained from castor beans, this oil draws moisture to the skin and protects against environmental pollutants. Castor oil is also used for sunburn, burns, cuts skin irritation, and is reputed to ease inflammation and muscle pains.

Evening primrose oil

Oenothera biennis

A pale yellow oil produced from the seeds of the evening primrose flower. High in GLA or omega-6, it helps to ease eczema, psoriasis and dry skin. This oil is easily absorbed and used in skin preparations, especially on the face to prevent premature ageing.

Flax seed (linseed) oil

Linum usitatissimum

A light brown oil high in the natural antioxidant vitamin E and omega-3 that provide valuable skin strengthening and nutritional properties. It is known for its anti-inflammatory properties which can help minimise the appearance of scars, stretch marks, redness, eczema, acne and psoriasis.

Hazelnut oil

Corylus americana

Grown in Northern Europe, hazelnut trees produce a vitamin-rich oil with excellent emollient properties, high levels of thiamine (vitamin B1) and vitamin B6. Hazelnut oil has long been used to treat dry and damaged skin and for filtering out the sun and thereby used in sun-care products.

Grapefruits

Macadamia nuts

Pomegranates

Grapefruit seed extract

Citrus grandis

Grapefruit seed extract is a thick dark liquid naturally derived from the seeds and pulp of the grapefruit. It is widely used as a way to naturally inhibit the growth of bacteria, and other organisms. The liquid form can be used in a scrub to help with skincare and preservation or to treat various skin conditions.

Kukui nut oil

Aleurites moluccana

Used in Hawaii for many years to rejuvenate, moisturize and nourish dry, mature and damaged skin. Kukui nut oil contains vitamins A, C, and E, providing antioxidants that protect the skin. It is a non-greasy oil effective in easing sunburn, eczema, psoriasis and dry sensitive skin.

Macadamia nut oil

Macadamia ternifolia

The oil is produced from the nuts of a native American tree. It contains high levels of palmitoleic acid, a substance similar to your skin's sebum – the skin's natural oil. Production of this sebum reduces naturally with time, resulting in drier skin as we age. Macadamia oil helps rejuvenate mature, dry skin, and aids stretch marks and burns.

Passionflower oil

Passiflora incarnata

Extracted from the fruit and seeds of the passionflower, this oil is high in linoleic acids and helps to restore the skin's elasticity. It is high in antioxidants and is a useful healing and antibacterial oil for dry itchy skin or scalp. Ideal for face preparations.

Pomegranate seed oil

Punica granatum

The seeds of the pomegranate fruit are packed full of antioxidants that fight free radicals and premature skin ageing. It is therefore used to aid regeneration of the skin cells helping to strengthen and nourish the epidermis and promote the skin's elasticity. The oil is also used to moisturize and heal dry, mature cracked skin, lines, wrinkles and sunburn.

Raspberry

Rice bran

Rose hip

Raspberry seed oil

Rubus idaeus

Extracted from the seeds of the raspberry fruit. Red raspberry seed oil is an excellent antioxidant, high in essential fatty acids and vitamin E which is important in the repair of skin damage. Its superior anti-inflammatory properties are particularly high making it effective in facial skin-care products, helping to soothe eczema, rashes and overheated, irritated skin. Raspberry seed oil also acts as a UV filter and is a valuable ingredient in sun-blocks and sun-screens. This is an expensive oil, but effective when used on the face in small amounts.

Rice bran oil

Oryza sativa

Extracted from the germ and inner husk of rice, rice bran oil is a mild and softening oil that has long been used in Japan to protect and moisturize mature or sensitive skin. High in essential fatty acids and Vitamin E it provides excellent antioxidant properties. Rich in oleic and linoleic acid, it is known to help inflammation, dry and ageing skin.

Rosemary extract

Rosmarinus officinalis

Rosemary extract is taken from the fragrant rosemary plant. It is rich in antioxidants and when added to scrubs can help to prolong the life of the product.

Rose hip oil

Rosa canina fruit oil or Rosa moschata

Obtained from the seeds of rose hips which contain high levels of vitamin E. Rose hip oil also contains retinol (vitamin A) which helps to delay the effects of skin ageing. It is widely used in skin-care products for its regenerating properties, and for helping dry, damaged, scarred skin, pigmentation and stretch marks. A perfect oil for face preparations.

St John's Wort

Strawberry seed oil

Fragaria vesca or Fragaria ananassa

Containing some of the most powerful sources of antioxidants found in nature, this luxurious oil is high in gamma tocopherol and is a valuable source of essential fatty acids such as linoleic, alpha-linoleic and oleic acid, making it a wonderful anti-ageing ingredient. Highly emollient, with a light texture and subtle aroma, it is also effective in soothing dry and damaged skin and is very useful in face preparations.

Wheatgerm

St John's Wort oil

Hypericum perforatum

A macerated oil, infused with St. John's Wort herb which is antiseptic, healing and pain-relieving. It is beneficial for nerve pain, neuralgia, sciatica, backache, shingles and lumbago. This oil is also used to sooth sunburn, burns, damaged skin, wounds and ulcers. It is a useful healing oil that can be used effectively in a poultice mask.

Vitamin E oil

Tocopherol

Fat-soluble antioxidants, found in a wide variety of fruit and vegetables, protect against cell-damaging free radicals, which are produced by pollution, fried food, smoking, stress, sunbathing, infection and stress. Vitamin E is also effective in reducing stretch marks, age spots, scars, dry ageing skin, keeping the skin looking younger. This oil is thick and viscous and should only be used in small amounts to enhance a product or to help with oxidisation.

Wheatgerm oil

Triticum vulgare

An emollient oil expressed from the germ of the wheat kernel, which is high in essential fatty acids, vitamins E, A, D, and linoleic acid (omega-6). The oil is used for dry, cracked skin and for its antioxidant properties which help to detoxify and protect the skin from environmental pollutants. A nourishing and skin-conditioning oil, which assists with the repair of sun-damaged, sensitive and dehydrated skin.

Recipes

Give yourself gorgeous skin with some of nature's most nurturing ingredients. Scrub your face or body with the delicious brown sugar and let the honey draw in moisture to leave your skin feeling soft and pampered.

Bee gorgeous

See pages 27–29 for basic instructions.

What you will need

3 tablespoons brown sugar
2 tablespoons (30ml) honey
2 tablespoons (30ml) sweet almond oil
2 tablespoons oat bran

Instructions

Place the ingredients in a bowl and mix together. Spoon into a storage container. To use, apply to damp skin on your face or body and gently exfoliate. Wash off with warm water, then moisturize.

Storage

Any leftovers can be stored in the refrigerator for several weeks.

Suitable for all skin types, this face mask is especially beneficial for dry or problem skin. The combination of hydrating, healing and antiseptic honey with the protein-rich egg yolk will give your skin a well-deserved boost.

Honey pie

See page 35 for basic instructions.

What you will need

1 tablespoon (15ml) manuka (or regular) honey
1 egg yolk
¼ teaspoon (1.25ml) borage (star flower) oil

Instructions

Whip the egg yolk with a small beater and add the remaining ingredients. Apply to your cleansed face, leave for 15 minutes, then wash off with warm water and moisturize.

Storage

Discard any remaining ingredients as this freshly-made mask will not keep.

The ground peach stones in this hand scrub provide excellent exfoliation while the peach oil regenerates and revitalizes the skin. Keep a jar by your kitchen sink and use weekly for silky smooth hands.

Peachy polish

See pages 28–29 for basic instructions.

What you will need

5oz (150g) light brown sugar
¾oz (25g) finely ground peach stones (apricot or olive)
4½oz (125g) peach oil (or sweet almond)
40 drops (2ml) peach fragrance oil

Note: If you have sensitive skin and prefer a gentle scrub, simply leave out the ground peach stones.

Instructions

Mix all the ingredients together in a bowl before transferring to a storage container. To use, massage into wet skin and wash off with warm water. If you are unable to obtain ground peach, almond or olive stones, just add an extra ¾oz (25g) of light brown sugar to the recipe for an equally fabulous scrub.

Storage

Any leftovers can be stored in the refrigerator for several weeks.

This poultice mask can be used to help heal minor ailments such as sprains, bruises, scars, inflamed skin or blemishes. You can tailor-make your own mask with different botanicals that are beneficial to your specific problem.

Healing herbal

See page 35 for basic instructions.

What you will need

3 tablespoons white clay
3 tablespoons bentonite clay
1 tablespoon ginseng powder
1 tablespoon chamomile powder
1 tablespoon comfrey root powder
Calendula oil – enough to mix to a smooth paste

Instructions

Put all the dry ingredients in a bowl and mix with a spoon or hand whisk. To use, mix to a paste with the calendula oil (or water) to activate the mask. Apply to clean skin, leave for 15 minutes, then wash off with warm water and moisturize.

Storage

The dry mixture will keep in an airtight container for 18 months.

Oily and blemished skin will benefit from this face and body sugar scrub. Citric acid in the lemon juice helps to clear spots and grease, honey is antibacterial and moisturizing, while olive oil nourishes your skin.

Spot the difference

See pages 27–29 for basic instructions.

What you will need

10½oz (300g) white sugar

3 tablespoons (45ml) lemon juice

2 tablespoons (30ml) olive oil

2 tablespoons (30ml) manuka (or regular) honey

Instructions

Mix all the ingredients together in a bowl, then transfer to a storage container. To use, massage into wet skin and wash off with warm water.

Storage

This face and body scrub can be stored for several weeks in a refrigerator.

Nature provides us with clays containing minerals, trace elements and nutrients which have a nourishing, restoring and soothing effect on the skin. This deep cleansing recipe helps to draw out toxins leaving skin toned and firm.

Earthworks

See page 35 for basic instructions.

What you will need

3 teaspoons Fuller's earth clay
3 teaspoons bentonite clay

For each face mask application add:
1 teaspoon (5ml) cow's or goat's milk

Note: This recipe is not for use on sensitive or very dry skin.

Instructions

Mix the Fuller's earth and bentonite clay in a bowl using a spoon or hand whisk. To use, mix approximately 1 teaspoon (5ml) of milk (or water) to 1 heaped teaspoon of dry mask to a paste. Apply to your cleansed face, leave for 15 minutes, then wash off with warm water and moisturize.

Storage

The dry mixture will keep in an airtight container for 18 months.

Scrub away those dead skin cells on your body with the concentrated mineral rich elements extracted from the Dead Sea itself. The high magnesium content helps to hydrate the skin and reduce inflammation.

Dead Sea spa

See pages 28–29 for basic instructions.

What you will need

17½oz (500g) Dead Sea salt
8¾oz (250g) olive oil (weighed)
1 tablespoon Dead Sea mud
½ teaspoon (2.5ml) rosemary essential oil
½ teaspoon (2.5ml) eucalyptus essential oil

Instructions

Mix all the ingredients together in a bowl, then transfer to a storage container. To use, massage into wet skin and wash off with warm water.

Storage

This scrub can be stored for several weeks in a refrigerator.

Dead Sea mud is packed with unique health benefits to enhance and restore the texture of your skin. It can help draw out impurities, reduce large pores, soften, tone and firm, giving a more youthful appearance.

Marvellous minerals

See page 35 for basic instructions.

What you will need

4 tablespoons white clay
4 tablespoons Dead Sea clay (powder)

For each face mask application add:
1 teaspoon (5ml) approximately brine (½ teaspoon Dead Sea salt dissolved in warm water) – enough to mix to a paste

Note: Wet Dead Sea mud can be used instead of dry clay. This can also be applied to the face as a mask on its own.

Instructions

Mix all the dry ingredients together with a spoon or hand whisk, then transfer to a storage container. To use, dissolve the salt in water and add to 1 heaped teaspoon of dry mixture. Mix to a thick paste. Apply to your cleansed face and leave for 15 minutes, wash off with warm water and moisturize.

Storage

The dry mixture will keep in an airtight container for 18 months.

Enhance, enrich and exfoliate your skin with these precious plant oils.
Rose geranium and patchouli condition the skin, while the almond and rose
hip oil help to reduce the appearance of stretch marks and scarring.

Enriching life

See pages 28–29 for basic instructions.

What you will need

17½ (500g) fine sea salt
6¾oz (190g) sweet almond oil (weighed)
1 tablespoon (15ml) rose hip oil
1½ teaspoons (7.5ml) rose geranium essential oil
½ teaspoon (2.5ml) patchouli essential oil

Instructions

Mix all the ingredients together in a bowl, then transfer
to a storage container. To use this body scrub, massage
into wet skin and wash off with warm water.

Storage

This can be stored for several months in a refrigerator.

The exotic properties of tropical fruits will soothe and soften dry sensitive skin. The deliciously fragrant fruits are packed with vitamins and minerals helping to aid restoration and rejuvenation of the skin's elasticity.

Rainforest

See page 35 for basic instructions.

What you will need

4 tablespoons white clay

2 tablespoons mango powder

1 tablespoon banana powder

2 tablespoons milk powder

1 tablespoon honey powder (optional)

For each face mask application add: 1 teaspoon (5ml) tropical fruit juice (pineapple, mango, orange). **Note:** If you are unable to find powders, simply mash fresh fruit and mix with honey.

Instructions

Mix all the dry ingredients together with a spoon or hand whisk, then transfer to a storage container. To use, mix approximately 1 teaspoon (5ml) of fruit juice (or water) to 1 heaped teaspoon of dry ingredients, mix to a paste and apply to your cleansed face. Leave for 15 minutes before washing off with warm water and moisturizing.

Storage

The dry mixture will keep in an airtight container for 18 months.

A toe-tingling foot scrub to stimulate your toes. Scrub away dead skin and moisturize at the same time. The essential oils are known to be antibacterial and anti-fungal leaving your feet feeling clean and fresh.

Playing footsie

See pages 28–29 for basic instructions.

What you will need

8¾oz (250g) sea salt

1 tablespoon green clay

4½oz (125g) sweet almond oil

20 drops (1ml) tea tree essential oil

20 drops (1ml) peppermint essential oil

2 tablespoons pumice powder (optional)

2 tablespoons shredded loofah (optional)

Note: Mix the pumice in thoroughly before application.

Instructions

Mix all the ingredients together in a bowl, then transfer to a storage container. To use, soak your feet in a bowl of warm water for 5–10 minutes, massage the scrub into wet skin, then wash off with warm water.

Storage

This scrub can be stored for several weeks in a refrigerator.

After an exfoliating foot scrub, use this foot mask to further soften and condition your feet. The lemon peel powder will leave your feet deodorized, delectable and ready for dancing.

Best foot forward

See pages 28–29 for basic instructions.

What you will need

3 tablespoons yellow clay
3 tablespoons white clay
1 tablespoon lemon peel powder (optional)

For each foot mask application add:
2 drops tea tree essential oil
2 drops lavender essential oil
1 tablespoon (15ml) approximately St John's Wort oil

Instructions

Mix all the dry ingredients together with a spoon or hand whisk, then transfer to a storage container. To use, mix approximately 1 tablespoon of dry mask ingredients to a paste with St John's Wort oil (or water) and essential oils. Apply to clean feet and upper legs, leave for 15 minutes, before washing off and moisturizing.

Storage

The dry mixture will keep in an airtight container for 18 months.

Use this soothing mask on your face, hands or any other area of the body that is dry and sensitive. The china clay will gently cleanse, while the milk lightly exfoliates old skin cells to leave it soft and supple.

China doll

See page 35 for basic instructions.

What you will need

12 tablespoons china (kaolin) white clay
6 tablespoons milk powder (or buttermilk/yoghurt/goat's milk)

For each face mask application add:
2 drops chamomile essential oil
1 teaspoon (5ml) approximately lavender water

Note: To use just on face only divide the main recipe by ¼.

Instructions

Mix all the dry ingredients together in a bowl with a spoon or hand whisk, then transfer to a storage container. To use, mix 1 teaspoon of dry mask ingredients to a paste with the lavender water (or water) and chamomile essential oil. Apply to cleansed skin, leave for 15 minutes, before washing off with warm water and moisturizing.

Storage

The dry mixture will keep in an airtight container for 18 months.

After a cold winter walk, thaw out your body and increase your circulation with this stimulating and warming body scrub. Then wrap up warm, curl up beside the fire and enjoy a steaming hot cup of cocoa.

Winter warmer

See pages 28–29 for basic instructions.

What you will need

2¾oz (80g) brown sugar

2¾oz (80g) olive oil (weighed)

1 teaspoon cinnamon powder

½ teaspoon (2.5ml) mandarin essential oil

10 drops ginger essential oil

10 drops black pepper essential oil

Note: Not reccomended for use on sensitive skin.

Instructions

Mix all the ingredients together in a bowl, then transfer to a storage container. To use, massage into wet skin and wash off with warm water.

Storage

This scrub can be stored for several weeks in a refrigerator.

Science tells us that rhassoul clay, from the Atlas mountains in Morocco, has unique absorption properties. It has been used since ancient Rome and Egyptian times for deep cleansing and conditioning of both skin and hair.

Science lesson

See page 35 for basic instructions.

What you will need

3 tablespoons rhassoul clay
3 tablespoons bentonite clay

For each face mask application add:
1 drop frankincense essential oil
1 drop lavender essential oil
1 teaspoon (5ml) approximately argan oil

Note: Not recommended for use on dry skin.

Instructions

Mix all the dry ingredients together with a spoon or hand whisk, then transfer to a storage container. To use, mix 1 teaspoon of the dry ingredients with argan oil (or water) and essential oils to a paste. Apply to your cleansed face and leave for 15 minutes, before washing off and moisturizing. The recipe can also be used as a hair and scalp mask, although you may need to double it.

Storage

The dry mixture will keep in an airtight container for 18 months.

Apart from being delicious to eat, chocolate is quickly becoming an important ingredient in cosmetics for its skin-softening and conditioning properties. Buff up your skin and see it shine with this sweet smelling body scrub.

Chocolate orange

See pages 28–29 for basic instructions.

What you will need

5oz (150g) dark brown sugar
1¾oz (50g) jojoba oil (weighed)
1 tablespoon organic cocoa powder
1 teaspoon (5ml) mandarin essential oil

Instructions

Mix all the ingredients together in a bowl, then transfer to a storage container. To use, massage into wet skin and wash off with warm water. Depending on the sugar used and your personal preference, you may wish to add a little more jojoba oil to the recipe.

Storage

This scrub can be stored for several weeks in a refrigerator.

Chocolate powder is high in antioxidants which help to slow damage to the skin caused by free radicals and pollutants. If this yummy mask accidentally slides onto your mouth, simply lick your lips and enjoy!

Chocolate truffle

See page 35 for basic instructions.

What you will need

2 tablespoons organic cocoa powder
1 tablespoon (15ml) runny honey
1 tablespoon (15ml) double cream

Instructions

Mix all the ingredients together in a small bowl. To use, apply to your cleansed face and leave 15 minutes before washing off with warm water and moisturizing.

Storage

This recipe will not keep so discard any leftover mixture.

A gentle scrub for use early in the morning. Oats are great for relieving irritated, itchy and inflamed skin and have long been used in skin-care preparations for the treatment of spots, acne and problem skin.

Breakfast time

See page 27 for basic instructions.

What you will need

6 tablespoons demerara sugar

6 tablespoons oats (finely ground)

Cow's or goat's milk – enough to mix to a smooth paste

Note: If you are using this recipe just for the face, divide the recipe by ⅓.

Instructions

Finely ground the oats in a food processor. Mix both the dry ingredients together in a bowl, then transfer to a storage container. To use, mix to a paste with the milk. Massage into wet skin on face or body, then wash off with warm water.

Storage

The dry mixture can be stored for several weeks in an air-tight container.

An inexpensive and quick face mask which uses ingredients from your refrigerator or kitchen cupboard. Each one is bursting with valuable vitamins and minerals known to smooth dry, wrinkled and ageing skin.

Country dairy

See page 35 for basic instructions.

What you will need

1 egg yolk
1 tablespoon (15ml) full fat Greek (or thick) yoghurt

Instructions

Mix the ingredients together in a small bowl. To use, apply to your cleansed face, leave 15 minutes, before washing off with warm water and moisturizing.

Storage

This face mask will not keep so discard any leftover mixture.

A great body scrub for toning, detoxing and for helping diminish cellulite. Epsom salts draw out toxins from the skin, while lemon and grapefruit are known for their revitalizing and stimulating properties.

Lemon grove

See pages 28–29 for basic instructions.

What you will need
8¾oz (250g) Epsom salts
3½oz (100g) sweet almond oil (weighed)
20 drops (1ml) lemon essential oil
20 drops (1ml) grapefruit essential oil

Instructions
Mix all the ingredients together in a bowl, then transfer to a storage container. To use, massage into wet skin and wash off with warm water.

Storage
This scrub can be stored for several weeks in a refrigerator.

There is nothing more delicious than the strawberry season. If you have one or two over-ripe fruits, why not use them to make yourself this quick cleansing, softening and refreshing face mask.

Strawberry cream

See page 36 for basic instructions.

What you will need

2 very ripe strawberries
1 tablespoon (15ml) thick cream
2 teaspoons (10ml) honey
2 tablespoons ground almonds

Instructions

Mash the ripe strawberries with a fork or hand blender until mushy, then mix in the rest of the ingredients. To use, apply to your cleansed face and leave for 15 minutes. Massage the mixture into the skin to give a gentle exfoliation, before washing off with warm water and moisturizing.

Storage

This face mask will not keep so discard any leftover mixture.

Nature has kindly given us wonderful facial exfoliants within a multitude of berries and fruits. Fruit seeds gently remove excess skin cells making way for fresh new cells to leave your skin looking radiant.

Berry good

See page 27 for basic instructions.

What you will need

3½oz (100g) white (kaolin) clay
2 teaspoons raspberry powder
3½oz (100g) raspberry seeds

Note: If you haven't got raspberry powder or seeds, you can substitute with cranberry or strawberry.

Instructions

Mix all the ingredients together in a bowl with a spoon or hand whisk, then transfer to a storage container. To use, mix a few tablespoons to a paste with water, milk or oil. Apply the scrub to your cleansed face and gently exfoliate, before washing off with warm water and moisturizing.

Storage

The dry mixture can be stored for upto 18 months.

Avocado and aloe are both highly moisturizing and nourishing. Together they make an effective face mask to restore mature, dehydrated or sun-damaged skin, or to relieve eczema or psoriasis.

Avocado & aloe

See page 36 for basic instructions.

What you will need

½ an over-ripe avocado pear

1 teaspoon (5ml) aloe vera juice (or gel)

Instructions

Mash the over-ripe avocado pear with a fork and mix with the aloe vera juice. To use, apply to your cleansed face, leave for 15 minutes, then wash off with warm water and moisturize.

Storage

This face mask will not keep, so discard any leftover mixture.

Fresh tomatoes and cucumber cleanse, refresh and cool your skin to leave it bright and refined. Ideal for use after digging in your vegetable plot on a hot summer's day, particularly if you have caught too much sun.

Veggie patch

See page 36 for basic instructions.

What you will need

½ tomato, finely chopped
¾oz (25g) cucumber, peeled and finely chopped
2 tablespoons ground almonds

Note: If you haven't got fresh tomatoes, use tomato juice or paste instead.

Instructions

Blend the tomato and cucumber with a hand blender until very mushy, then add the ground almonds. To use, apply to your cleansed face and leave for 15 minutes. Massage the mixture into your skin for a gentle exfoliation, before washing off with warm water and moisturizing.

Storage

This mask will not keep so discard any leftover mixture.

Green tea contains powerful antioxidants and vitamins which assist in the repair of cell damage, wrinkles and blemishes. Drinking green tea and using a green tea face mask can keep your skin looking youthful and healthy.

Green tea

See page 35 for basic instructions.

What you will need

3 tablespoons white (kaolin) clay
2 tablespoons green clay
1 teaspoon green tea powder

For each face mask application add:
1 teaspoon (5ml) approximately rice bran oil

Instructions

Mix all the dry ingredients together in a bowl with a spoon or hand whisk, then transfer to a storage container. To use, mix 1 heaped teaspoon of the dry mask to a paste with the rice bran oil (alternatively with water). Apply to your cleansed face and leave for 15 minutes, before washing off with water and moisturizing.

Storage

The dry mixture can be stored for upto 18 months.

The smell of coffee is invigorating and stimulating, so a caffeine-fuelled body scrub is sure to set you up for the day. Caffeine helps to firm and tighten your skin, diminishing redness and reducing the appearance of cellulite.

Espresso

See page 27 for basic instructions.

What you will need

2¾oz (80g) coffee grounds
2¾oz (80g) dark brown sugar
7oz (200g) hempseed (olive or sweet almond) oil

Instructions

Mix all the ingredients together in a bowl, then transfer to a storage container. To use, massage into wet skin, then wash off with warm water.

Storage

This scrub can be stored for several weeks in a refrigerator.

Pink and white clay are very gentle, ideal for sensitive or delicate skin.
Rose hips are rich in natural vitamin C, great for firming and toning
your face, as well as helping to protect your skin from capillary damage.

Delicate flower

See page 35 for basic instructions.

What you will need

2 tablespoons pink clay
I tablespoon white (kaolin) clay
½ teaspoon rose hip powder
I tablespoon honey powder (optional)

For each face mask application add:
I teaspoon (5ml) approximately evening primrose oil
I drop chamomile essential oil
I drop rose geranium essential oil

Instructions

Mix all the dry ingredients together with a spoon or hand whisk, then transfer to a storage container. To use, mix I heaped teaspoon of dry ingredients with the evening primrose oil (or water) and the essential oils and mix to a paste. To use, apply to your cleansed face and leave for 15 minutes, before washing off and moisturizing.

Storage

The dry mixture can be stored for upto 18 months.

Vitamin E and beta-carotene (from carrots) are antioxidants which help to restore and protect sun-damaged skin. With a shot of vitamin C from the limes, this energizing body scrub should give you a great vitamin boost.

Vitamin body buffer

See pages 28–29 for basic instructions.

What you will need

10½oz (300g) sea salt
3 ½oz (100g) grapeseed oil (olive or sweet almond oil)
1 teaspoon (5ml) vitamin E oil
1 teaspoon (5ml) carrot tissue oil
1 teaspoon (5ml) lime essential oil (or fresh lime/lemon juice)

Instructions

Mix all the ingredients together in a bowl, then transfer to a storage container. To use, massage into wet skin and wash off with warm water.

Storage

This scrub can be stored for several weeks in a refrigerator.

Provide your face with a feast of goodness from health-giving fresh fruit, honey and olive oil. A thoroughly moisturizing and nourishing face mask to feed your face when it needs some tender loving care.

Facial feast

See page 36 for basic instructions.

What you will need

½ an over-ripe banana
¼ an over-ripe avocado pear
1 teaspoon (5ml) honey
1 teaspoon (5ml) extra virgin olive oil

Instructions

Mash the over-ripe banana and over-ripe avocado pear with a fork or a hand blender. Add the honey and olive oil, then mix to a smooth paste. To use, apply to your cleansed face and leave for 15 minutes, before washing off with warm water and moisturizing.

Storage

This recipe will not keep, so discard any leftover mixture.

This luxury spa treatment is the ultimate in mineral-rich goodness and detoxification for your skin and body. The Dead Sea salt and clay have numerous benefits to leave your skin in tip-top condition.

It's a wrap

See page 35 for basic instructions.

What you will need

5oz (150g) bentonite clay
1¾oz (50g) Dead Sea salt (Epsom or sea salt)
9oz (225ml) hot water
2 tablespoons (30ml) sweet almond oil (or olive)

Note: If you have any cuts or scrapes leave out the Dead Sea salts, and just use water, as the salt will sting.

Instructions

Dissolve the salt in hot water and add to the clay and almond oil. Use only enough to make a thick smooth paste – add more warm water if necessary. To use, stand in an empty bath and apply to your face and body. Wrap yourself with a foil blanket, thin towels or sheets and lie in the bath for a minimum of 45 minutes, then shower off the mask.

Storage

This recipe will not keep, so discard any leftover mixture.

Conversions

The tables below are a general guide for the measurements used throughout the book. Please note that the imperial measurements are approximate conversions from the metric.

When following the instructions, use either the metric or the imperial measurements, do not mix units. For practical reasons, measurements below one millilitre have been left as drops only.

Volume

20 drops = 1ml	1 teaspoon = 5ml	1oz = 30ml
40 drops = 2ml	2 teaspoons = 10ml	2oz = 60ml
60 drops = 3ml	1 tablespoon = 15ml	3oz = 85ml
80 drops = 4ml	2 tablespoons = 30ml	4oz = 120ml
100 drops = 5ml		5oz = 140ml

Dry weights

1oz = 30g
2oz = 60g
3oz = 90g
4oz = 120g
5oz = 150g

Suppliers and resources

Europe

Amphora Aromatics
www.Amphora-aromatics.com
Cotham, Bristol
Tel: +44 (0) 117 904 7212
Wide range of essential oils, oils and
aromatherapy supplies and carrier oils.

Aromantic Ltd
www.aromantic.co.uk
Forres, Moray
Tel: +44 (0) 1309 696 900
Good range of cosmetic ingredients,
oils, exfoliants and clays.

G. Baldwin & Co
www.baldwins.co.uk
London
Tel: +44 (0) 20 7703 5550
Herbs, essential oils, carrier oils, clays,
macerated oils and flower essences.

Gracefruit
www.gracefruit.com
Longcroft, Stirlingshire
Tel: +44 (0) 141 416 2906
Oils, clays, exfoliants, and an excellent
range of dried fruit powders, honey
powder, yoghurt and milk powders.

Infusions Ltd
www.infusions4chefs.co.uk
Bury St Edmunds, Suffolk
Tel: +44 (0) 1359 272 577
Email: info@infusions4chefs.co.uk
An ingredients company for chefs
supplying a good range of fruit powders.

Just A Soap
www.justasoap.co.uk
Whepstead, Bury St Edmunds
Tel: +44 (0) 1284 735 043
Clays and exfoliants.

New Directions (UK)
www.newdirectionsUK.com
Fordingbridge, Hampshire,
Tel: +44 (0) 1425 655 555
Email: info@newdirectionsUK.com
Oils, essential oils, herbal extracts, fruit
powders, exfoliants, clays, wide range of
bottles, jars and containers.

New Directions (Portugal)
www.newdirections.com.pt
Lisboa, Portugal
Tel: +351 21 393 2230/6
Email: geral@newdirections.com.pt

Plush Folly
Hampton, Middlesex
Tel: +44 (0) 7851 429 957
Email: info@plushfolly.com
Fruit powders including tomato,
honey powder, clays and minerals.

Sheabutter Cottage
www.sheabuttercottage.co.uk
Sonning, Reading
Tel: +44 (0) 118 969 3830
Exotic and fair trade oils, essential oils,
clays, honey powder, and other ethically-
sourced ingredients.

Soap Basics
www.soapbasics.co.uk
Melksham, Wiltshire
Tel: +44 (0) 1225 899 286
E-mail: info@soapbasics.co.uk
Fragrances, herbs, oils, clays, exfoliants.

Thermae Bath Spa
Bath, Wiltshire
Tel: +44 (0) 844 888 0844 or
+44 (0)1225 33 1234
Healing waters for relaxation and
pampering.

The Soap Kitchen

www.thesoapkitchen.co.uk

Torrington, Devon

Tel: +44 (0)1805 622 944

Email: info@thesoapkitchen.co.uk

All the ingredients you need to make the recipes in this book. Oils, herbs, containers and bottles. Fragrances, essential oils, exfoliants, clays and fruit powders.

The Soapmakers Store

www.soapmakers-store.com

Horsham, West Sussex

Tel: + 44 (0) 844 800 3386

Many cosmetic ingredients, including oils, essential oils, clays and exfoliants.

Australia and New Zealand

Aussie Soap Supplies

www.aussiesoapsupplies.com.au

Palmyra WA 6957

Tel: (08) 9339 1885

Email: david@aussiesoapsupplies.com.au

Oils, cosmetic ingredients, exfoliants and interesting blends of Australian clays.

Essential Oils and Soap

www.oilsandsoap.com.au

Beaconsfield TAS 7270

Tel: (03) 6394 3737

Email: info@oilsandsoap.com.au

Oils, clays and exfoliants.

Heirloom Body Care

www.heirloombodycare.com.au

Llandilo NSW 2747

Tel: (02) 4777 4457

Email: heirloom@heirloombodycare.com.au

Oils, clays, exfoliants good range of cosmetic packaging, and many other supplies.

New Directions

www.newdirections.com.au

Sydney, Australia

Tel: 61 2 8577 5999

Toll Free: 1800 637 697

Email: nda@newdirections.com.au

Huge range of ingredients including oils, essential oils, excellent range of bottles and jars. Extensive range of exfoliants, clays, mud, volcanic ash and fruit powders.

Manuka Oil.com

www.manukaoil.com

Bio-Extracts Limited.

South Auckland, New Zealand.

Phone: +64 9 236 0917

Email: email@ManukaOil.com

Manuka essential oil.

USA & Canada

Bramble Berry Inc.
www.brambleberry.com
Bellingham, WA 98225
Tel: 360/734-8278
Toll Free: 877-627-7883
Huge range of ingredients, oils, fragrances, essential oils, exfoliants, clays and oils.

Camden-Grey Essential Oils Inc.
www.camdengrey.com
3579 NW 82 Ave.
Doral, FL 33122
Toll Free Line for orders only:
866-503-8615
Tel: 305-500-9630
Fax: 305-500-9425
Email: orderdesk@camdengrey.com
Wide range of oils, essential oils, exfoliants and clays.

Cranberry Lane
www.cranberrylane.com
Richmond, BC
Toll-Free: 1-800-833-4533
Local: 604-944-1488
Good supply of most ingredients.

From Nature With Love
www.fromnaturewithlove.com
Natural Sourcing, LLC
Oxford, CT 06478
Tel: (800) 520-2060 or (203) 267-6061
Extensive range of ingredients; fruit seed exfoliants, good range of clays and mud.

Herbal Accents
www.herbalaccents.com
Alpinie, CA 91903-0937
Tel: 619-562-2650
Email: sales@herbalaccents.com
Good range of ingredients including exfoliants, fruit seeds and clays.

Just Tomatoes, Etc.!
www.justtomatoes.com
Westley, CA 95387
Tel: (800) 537-1985
Local: (209) 894-5371
Email: customerservice@justtomatoes.com
A company specializing in fruit powders and organic fruit powders.

Kangaroo Blue
www.kangarooblue.com
Plainfield, IL 60585
Tel: 815-609-9275
Local: 815-609-9275
Oils, essential oils, Australian clays and salts.

Mountain Rose Herbs
www.mountainroseherbs.com
Eugene, OR 97405
Tel: (800) 879-3337
International: (541) 741 7307
Certified organic herb specialists, good range of oils, clays and salts, essential oils and bottles.

Majestic Mountain Sage
www.thesage.com (look under Catalog)
Logan, Utah 84321
Tel: 435-755-0863
Oils, clays, fruit seeds and exfoliants.

New Directions Aromatics (USA)
www.newdirectionsaromatics.com
San Ramon, CA 94583
Tel: 1-800-246-7817 (Toll Free)
Email: sales@newdirectionsaromatics.com
Huge range of ingredients including an extensive selection of fruit powders and exfoliants, oils, essential oils, excellent range of bottles and jars.

New Directions Aromatics (Canada)

www.newdirectionsaromatics.ca
Ontario, Canada
Tel: 905-840-5459
Order Desk: 1-877-255-7692 (Toll-free)
Email: oils@newdirectionsaromatics.ca
Huge range of ingredients including an extensive selection of fruit powders and exfoliants, oils, essential oils, excellent range of bottles and jars.

The Chemistry Store

www.chemistrystore.com
Cayce, SC 29033
Toll Free: 800-224-1430
Email sales: sales@chemistrystore.com
Email order Inquires:
glitter@chemistrystore.com
Salts, clays and exfoliants.

The Essential Oil Company

www.essentialoil.com
Portland, Oregon 97202
Toll Free: 800-729-5912
Local: 503-872-8735
Organic, wildcrafted and cultivated essential oils and oils.

The Scent Works

www.Scent-Works.com
Durham, North Carolina
Tel: 1-973-598-9600
Email sales: TheScentworks.com
Oils, fragrance & essential oils, herbs, and containers.

Snowdrift Farm, Inc.

www.snowdriftfarm.com
Tucson, AZ 85713 USA
Tel: 520-882-7080
Toll Free: 888-999-6950
Wide range of all ingredients, including salts, clays and exfoliants.

About the author

Elaine Stavert formed The Littlecote Soap Co. after a life-changing move from her television career in London to a farm in the beautiful Buckinghamshire countryside. Surrounded by hedgerows and meadows, and with a keen interest in herbalism and aromatherapy, Elaine was soon developing a range of natural toiletries, bath products and candles that were eco-friendly, kind to the skin and quintessentially English. Elaine's passion for her products is evident in the pure and natural ingredients that she uses in imaginative ways to produce traditional recipes with contemporary twists.

The Littlecote Soap Co., Littlecote Farm, Littlecote, Nr Dunton, Buckingham, MK18 3LN United Kingdom.
www.littlecotesoap.co.uk

Acknowledgements

Robert, Diane and Pearl
For love, encouragement, patience and support.

I would also like to thank my wonderful team at The Littlecote Soap Co., Caroline Heron, Nikki Jellis, Rebecca Gulliver, Andrea Ellis, Alison Vinter, Carole Capel, Jess Bliss, Diane Winks, Pearl Olney, Sean Jackman and Mr Nab. Also beauty therapist Clair Smith, Immy, Millie and Rosie Smith, beekeepers Jonathan and Rebecca Longley, Charlotte Hanna from The Thermae Bath Spa, and finally, Benjamin Hedges without whom the company would not exist.

My thanks also to the talented team at GMC Publications; to Jonathan Bailey and Gerrie Purcell for inviting me to write this book, to Beth Wicks for her editing skills, professionalism and patience, and to Rob Janes, Rebecca Mothersole and Gilda Pacitti for their creative eye for detail and design.

Picture acknowledgements

Main photography and page 14 by Rebecca Mothersole.
Step-by-step photographs by Elaine Stavert.

Wikimedia Commons: **Page 10** *Cleopatra Testing Poisons on Condemned Prisoners*, Alexander Cabanel, 1887/Celithemis; **Page 11, top** Toilet box and various vessels of Merit/Jean-Pierre Dalbera; **Page 11, bottom** Gazelle-shaped kohl spoon/Rama; **Page 12** Aarti in Varanasi/orvalrochefort; **Page 13, left** Széchenyi Gyógyfürdö thermal spa in Budapest/Aida; **Page 13, right** Women bath Asteas/Jastrow; **Page 15** Alma-Tadema Strigils and sponges/juanpdp; **Page 16** Plan of the Old Baths at Pompeii by Overbeck/Sandstein; **Page 17, top left** Roman Baths c1900/NotFromUtrecht; **Page 17, top right** Bladud Statue at Roman Baths, Bath/Smalljim; **Page 17, bottom** Caldarium/Mschlindwein; **Page 18** Blue Lagoon 3/SketchUp; **Page 19** Kneippkur/Frumpy

Index

Names of recipes are given in italics

To place an order, or to request a catalogue, contact:

GMC Publications Ltd

Castle Place, 166 High Street, Lewes, East Sussex, BN7 1XU

Tel: +44 (0)1273 488005 **Website:** www.gmcbooks.com

Orders by credit card are accepted